Humanity, Diversity, and the Liberal Arts
Foundation of a College Education

Joseph B. Cuseo
Emeritus Marymount College

Aaron Thompson
Eastern Kentucky University

Kendall Hunt
publishing company

Book Team

Chairman and Chief Executive Officer   Mark C. Falb
President and Chief Operating Officer   Chad M. Chandlee
Vice President, Higher Education   David L. Tart
Director of Publishing Partnerships   Paul B. Carty
Editorial Manager   Georgia Botsford
Senior Developmental Editor   Lynnette M. Rogers
Vice President, Operations   Timothy J. Beitzel
Assistant Vice President, Production Services   Christine E. O'Brien
Senior Production Editor   Charmayne McMurray
Permissions Editor   Renae Horstman
Cover Designer   Jeni Chapman

Cover image © 2010, Shutterstock, Inc.

Kendall Hunt
publishing company

www.kendallhunt.com
Send all inquiries to:
4050 Westmark Drive
Dubuque, IA 52004-1840

Printed in the United States of America
10 9 8 7 6 5 4 3 2

Contents

◆ Preface

◆ Purpose and Plan of This Book

This book is designed to serve three primary purposes:

- **Motivational**: Inspire and excite you about your upcoming college experience, particularly the part of it that you will experience most intensively during your first two years: the liberal arts and general education.

- **Organizational**: Provide the "big picture"—an overview for making sense of the total college experience that will allow you to see the forest as well as the trees.

- **Preparatory**: Supply a sneak preview of what is ahead of you, so that you can develop a long-range plan for doing college strategically—right from the start.

Preview of Content

Chapter 1. Liberal Arts: The Meaning and Purpose of General Education

This chapter will help you gain a deeper understanding and appreciation of the liberal arts—the core component of the college experience and the essence of a college education—which provide you with a powerful set of transferable skills for success in all college majors, careers, and life roles. You will learn how the liberal arts will broaden your perspective on the whole world, develop yourself as a whole person, and enrich the overall quality (and marketability) of your college education. The chapter ends with an action plan for making the most of general education by making effective use of the *total* college environment, including both the curriculum *and* co-curriculum—i.e., learning inside and outside the classroom.

Chapter 2. Diversity and Its Relationship to the Liberal Arts

This chapter clarifies what "diversity" really means, how it embraces all of humanity and benefits all people, and how it further broadens the perspectives developed by the liberal arts. Simply stated, we learn more from diverse perspectives than we do from similar perspectives. Ignoring or blocking out the experiences and ideas of others who are unfamiliar to us is not only a poor social skill; it's also a poor learning strategy, particularly for the twenty-first century. The liberal arts and diversity combine to ensure that you acquire stable, yet flexible skills needed for lifelong success in a fast-changing world. The chapter ends with an action plan for infusing diversity into your college experience and integrating it with the liberal arts.

Chapter 3. The Benefits of Experiencing the Liberal Arts and Diversity

Chapters 1 and 2 address two questions: *What* are the liberal arts and diversity? *How* can they be used to enrich my educational and personal development? Chapter 3 addresses the question: *Why* are they critical for my success in college and beyond? This chapter pulls together all the major advantages of experiencing a college education that is infused with the liberal arts and diversity, such as improved performance in your chosen major and future career, increased self-awareness and self-confidence, and preparation for multiple life roles beyond college.

By finishing the book with a clear sense of the wide-ranging benefits of the liberal arts and diversity, you are more likely to take action on the strategies suggested throughout the book and use them throughout your college experience.

Process and Style of Presentation

How information is delivered is just as important as *what* information is delivered. When writing this text, we made an intentional attempt to deliver our message in a way that would:

- Stimulate your interest in learning,
- Increase the depth of your learning, and
- Strengthen your retention (memory) for what you have learned.

We attempted to do this by incorporating the following principles of motivation, learning, and memory throughout the text.

- At the *start* of each chapter, we begin with a **Reflection** question to activate or "turn on" your thoughts and feelings about the upcoming topic. This pre-reading exercise is designed to energize and orient your mind so that it is ready to make connections between the ideas and experiences that you already have in your head with those that you are about to encounter in the chapter. This instructional strategy implements one of the most powerful principles of human learning: we learn most effectively by relating what we are going to learn to what we have already learned and stored in our brain.

- Interspersed throughout each chapter are additional **Reflections** that ask you to stop and think about the material you are reading for your personal life. These periodic pauses keep you alert and mentally active throughout the reading process; this serves to intercept the "attention drift" that normally takes place when the brain continually receives and processes information

"JUNIOR'S WRITING HAS IMPROVED. HIS LETTERS FROM COLLEGE, PLEADING FOR MORE MONEY, ARE FORCEFULLY AND FLAWLESSLY WRITTEN."

Writing promotes deeper learning and thinking.

for an extended period of time—as it does while reading. The reflections will also deepen your understanding of the material you read because you are *writing* in response to what you are learning. Writing while you read encourages more active thinking and deeper learning than passively underlining or highlighting sentences.

- **Journal Entries** and **Exercises** are included at the *end* of each chapter that ask you to reflect further on the knowledge you acquired from the reading and transform that knowledge into informed action. As discussed in the body of this book, wisdom is not achieved by simply acquiring knowledge, but by actually doing something with the knowledge you've acquired—i.e., *applying* it or putting it into practice.

"One must learn by doing. For though you think you know, you have no certainty until you try."

–Sophocles, ancient Greek philosopher

The strategic positioning of Reflection questions at the beginning of the chapter, during the chapter, and at the end of the chapter, will combine to create an effective learning sequence that keeps you actively involved throughout the reading process—from start to finish.

- In each chapter, information is delivered through a variety of communication formats that include visual diagrams, relevant cartoons, advice from current and former college students, words of wisdom from famous and influential people, and personal experiences drawn from the authors' lives. Using multiple communicate channels to deliver information allows you to receive it through multiple sensory modalities (input channels), which enables your brain to store it in multiple sites. This deepens learning by allowing your brain to make multiple connections with the information being learned and strengthens your memory for it by laying down multiple memory tracks (traces).

Here is a complete and more detailed list of the book's key learning and motivational features.

Quotes

In the side margins you will find a wide variety of quotes that relate to and reinforce the ideas being discussed at that point in the chapter. These quotes come from highly accomplished individuals who have lived in different historical periods and who have specialized in a wide variety of fields, such as, philosophy and religion, the arts and sciences, business, politics, and athletics. The wide-ranging timeframes, cultures, and fields of study represented by the people who are quoted serve as testimony to the eternal and universal wisdom of their words, as well as the enduring and pervasive power of the liberal arts and diversity. A lot can be learned from the first-hand experiences shared by "real people." It is our hope that the words of these successful and highly regarded individuals will inspire you to enact their words of wisdom and aspire to reach the level of success and respect they have attained.

Student Perspectives

Throughout the book, you will find comments and advice from students at different stages of the college experience, including college graduates (alumni). Studies show that students can learn a great deal from their peers, especially from those who have "been there and done that"—i.e., peers who have experienced what you are about to experience. You can learn from both their reported success stories and stumbling blocks.

Personal Experiences

Each chapter contains personal experiences drawn from the authors' lives. We share experiences we had as college students, as professors working with college students as course instructors and academic advisors, and our life experiences. Personal stories can deepen learning and strengthen retention of the message or lesson contained in the story. We share our personal experiences with you for the purpose of personalizing the book and giving you the opportunity to learn from our experiences—even if it's learning not to make the same mistakes we made!

Concept Maps: Verbal-Visual Aids

The book contains a variety of concept (idea) maps that organize key points into visual form. When concepts are represented in a visual-spatial format, you are more likely to retain them because two different memory traces are recorded in your brain: verbal (words) and visual (images).

Cartoons: Emotional-Visual Aids

You will find cartoons appearing occasionally in the text. These attempts at humor are intended to provide you with a little entertainment, but, more importantly, to strengthen your retention of the concept depicted in the cartoon—by reinforcing it with a visual image (drawing) and an emotional experience (humor). If the cartoon manages to trigger at least a snicker, your body will release adrenalin—a hormone that facilitates memory formation; and if the cartoon actually generates a little laughter, it's likely to stimulate release of endorphins—natural, morphine-like chemicals in the brain that lower stress (and elevate mood!).

Research and Scholarly Support

The book's ideas and recommendations are grounded in research and scholarship drawn from a variety of academic fields. You will find references cited regularly throughout the book and a sizable reference section at the end of the book. You will also find that the references cited represent a balanced blend of older, "classic" scholarship and more recent "cutting edge" research. This variety of fields and times highlights the wide-ranging relevance of the ideas being discussed and points to their ability to withstand the test of time. It also underscores the fact that the subject of this book, like any other specific academic field or discipline, is built on a solid body of knowledge research and scholarship.

Acknowledgments

This book would never have been written if it were not for the influence of the following people on my philosophy of education. I thank Dr. Thomas Denver Wood, first and foremost, president of Marymount College (California), for teaching me about the dangers of narrow specialization ("doctoritis" as he derisively described it) and for alerting me to the practical power of a liberating arts ("education for survival" as he liked to call it). Thanks also to my esteemed faculty colleagues with whom I've shared many cross-disciplinary conversations in our common office wing and many interdisciplinary team-teaching experiences over the years, namely: Dr. Charles Dock (biology), Dr. Pam Schachter (sociology), Dr. John Perkins (philosophy), Dr. Allen Franz (anthropology), and Dr. Nancy Sanders (English and literature). This book reflects more than a quarter-of-a-century's worth of professional experiences at an authentically student-centered college that delivered a liberal arts education which fostered the appreciation of human diversity and the unity of our shared humanity.

Joe Cuseo

My Leadership Statement that I have posted on my office wall in part says "I believe that through study and life experience, individuals have opportunities to enrich their knowledge and refine their attitudes which are essential in acting responsibly. I believe in social justice and value those willing to utilize their talents assisting others in obtaining equitable justice. I believe in exercising power appropriately and strive to view all items in a critical and creative manner . . . ." These are core values of mine that would not exist without a strong liberal arts baseline. There have been many individuals (so many that I cannot name them all) who assisted me in obtaining that base, especially in the area of understanding the importance of thinking and reflecting that thought through the spoken and written word. However, my mother was the first who sat with me and taught me the value of listening, thinking, writing and speaking. She always said "boy you have two ears and one mouth, listen twice more than you speak." Many teachers like Donna Roberts (my high school senior English and speech teacher and School Newspaper Advisor) and college professors like Dr. Reid Luhman (Sociology), Dr. Edith Williams (English), Dr. Frank Williams (Philosophy) and Dr. Doris Wilkerson (one of my Ph.D Advisors) built on the base started by my mother. A Liberal Arts education is an education that keeps on giving. This is still clear today in my life with writing partners like Joe who has a wonderful intellect and great humor meshed with superior thinking skills and creative ways to express those in written and verbal form. Thanks Joe, for the opportunity to share our love for Liberal Arts and how diversity is woven within them.

Aaron Thompson

About the Authors

Joe Cuseo holds a Ph.D in educational psychology and assessment from the University of Iowa. Currently, he is professor emeritus of psychology at Marymount College (California) where for more than twenty-five years he directed the first-year seminar—taken by all new students. He is a columnist for a bimonthly newsletter published by the National Resource Center for the First-Year Experience and Students in Transition, and has received the resource center's "outstanding first-year advocate award." He is a fourteen-time recipient of the "faculty member of the year award" on his home campus, a student-driven award based on effective teaching and academic advising. He has made over one hundred presentations at college campuses and conferences across the country, and has authored articles, chapters, and books on the first-year experience, academic advising, student diversity, and the senior-year experience.

Aaron Thompson, Ph.D, is the interim vice president of academic affairs at the Kentucky Council on Postsecondary Education and a professor of sociology in the Department of Educational Leadership and Policy Studies at Eastern Kentucky University. Thompson has a Ph.D in sociology in areas of organizational behavior, race, and gender relations. Thompson has researched, taught, and/or consulted in areas of assessment, diversity, leadership, ethics, research methodology and social statistics, multicultural families, race and ethnic relations, student success, first-year students, retention, and organizational design. He is nationally recognized in the areas of educational attainment, academic success, and cultural competence. Dr. Thompson has worked in a variety of capacities within the two-year and four-year institutions. He got his start in college teaching within a community college. His latest co-authored books are *Diversity and the College Experience*, *Thriving in College and Beyond: Research-Based Strategies for Academic Success and Personal Development*, *Focus on Success*, and *Black Men and Divorce*. His upcoming books are *Infusing Diversity into Education: Research-Based Strategies for Appreciating and Learning Human Differences*, *Thriving in the Community College and Beyond*, and *Changing Student*

Culture from the Ground Up. He has more than thirty publications and numerous research and peer reviewed presentations. Thompson has traveled over the U.S. and has given more than five hundred workshops, seminars and invited lectures in areas of race and gender diversity, living an unbiased life, overcoming obstacles to gain success, creating a school environment for academic success, cultural competence, workplace interaction, organizational goal setting, building relationships, the first-year seminar, and a variety of other topics. He has been or is a consultant to educational institutions, corporations, non-profit organizations, police departments, and other governmental agencies.

Introduction

The "Blind Men and the Elephant" is an old Indian parable about a group of blind men who were touching an elephant to understand what the animal looked like. Each man touched a separate part of the elephant (e.g., trunk, tail, and body), but no man touched the whole elephant. When the blind men got together later to discuss their understanding of the elephant's appearance, none of them agreed, because each of them was influenced (and biased) by the particular part he had touched; none of them had the broader experience of touching all the parts to get an integrated and accurate perspective into the elephant's total being.

Using the elephant to symbolize your college education, this book is designed to help you see the "whole elephant." Its purpose to give you a sense of the "big picture" or the total jigsaw puzzle before you get involved (or get lost) with handling all its particular pieces. It will articulate how the liberal arts—the broad set of courses that you will experience most commonly during the first two years of your college education, will provide the general context and framework for making sense of your entire college experience, and equip you with deep and durable skills that serve as the foundation for your success in college and beyond.

This book will also demonstrate that the benefits of the liberal arts are magnified when they are infused with diversity. Learning about and from diverse cultures reinforces the mind-expanding influence of the liberal arts by enabling you to view issues from a multitude of perspectives. Just as experiencing the diverse disciplines (academic fields) in the liberal arts liberates you from narrow, egocentric (self-centered) thinking, experiencing diverse cultural perspectives liberates you from the tunnel vision of ethnocentric (culture-centered) thinking. Your experiences with the liberal arts and diversity complement one other; they work together to enable you to see the common *theme* (humanity) and the variations on that *theme* (diversity). As a result, you develop a broader, more complete understanding of yourself and the world around you.

You will also learn that there are very *practical* benefits of experiencing the liberal arts and diversity. They will combine to supply you with the key skills and perspectives needed to succeed in today's increasingly diverse and global economy. A global perspective, breadth of knowledge, and the ability to understand cross-cultural differences are skills that have become critical for career access and success. These are the very skills and developed by the liberal arts and diversity.

Studies show that college students, as well as their parents, are very interested (and concerned) about majors and careers, but they overlook, underrate, and underestimate the importance of the liberal arts for career success (72, 129, 164).

They often believe the "liberal arts" are something idealistic or impractical that cannot be put to use in the "real world" and will not help you get a "real job" (72). As a result, liberal arts courses are sometimes seen by students as unnecessary requirements they must "get out of the way" before they "get into" what is really important—their specialized major. This narrow viewpoint probably stems from two sources: (a) lack of knowledge about what the liberal arts actually stand for and are designed to do, and (b) misinterpretation of general education—a term often used interchangeably with the liberal arts—as something very "general" (non-specific) and without any particular value or practical purpose. As you will learn, this is far from the truth. This book will clearly document and demonstrate the practical advantages of the liberal arts—for your major, your career, and your personal life. Indeed, one of the major goals of this book is to capitalize on the practical skills developed by the liberal arts and diversity to promote both your success in college and your career success beyond college.

In addition to helping you understand *why* the liberal arts and diversity are essential to being a well-rounded, well-educated person who is well prepared for the twenty-first-century, this book provides you with suggestions on *how* to do it. It offers research-based recommendations for developing a systematic plan and a set of specific strategies for integrating the liberal arts and diversity into your college experience to maximize their impact on your personal development and future success.

Compared to your previous schooling, college will provide you with a broader range of course choices, more resources to capitalize on, more educational freedom, and more decision-making opportunities. Your own college experience will differ from any other college student. This freedom gives the opportunity to shape and create a college experience and a final college transcript is unlike any other college student—one that is uniquely your own and that will maximize your prospects for future success.

A well-planned college education infused with the liberal arts and diversity will supply you with the seeds for lifelong growth. By devising an early plan for planting those seeds strategically, you ensure that your investment in college will yield the greatest personal growth and have the greatest impact on your future success. This book will help you create that plan.

Enjoy the greater academic freedom you have in college, but employ it to your advantage—use it strategically to make the most of your college experience and college degree.

CHAPTER 1

Liberal Arts
The Meaning and Purpose of General Education

Reflection 1.1

Before you start reading this chapter, do your best to answer the question below. **Note:** This is not a test. (Repeat: This is not a test.)

Which one of the following statements do you think represents the most accurate meaning of the term *liberal arts*?

1. Learning to be less politically conservative.
2. Learning to be more artistic.
3. Learning about ideas rather acquiring practical skills.
4. Learning to spend money freely.
5. Learning skills for freedom.

(You will find the answer to this question later in the chapter.)

What Is the *Meaning* and *Purpose* of the Liberal Arts?

If you're uncertain about what the term "liberal arts" means, you're not alone. Most first-year students don't have a clear idea about what the liberal arts actually represent (73). If they were to guess, they might mistakenly say that it's something "impractical" or, perhaps, something to do with liberal politics—as illustrated by the following experience.

PERSONAL EXPERIENCE | Joe Cuseo

I was once advising a first-year student who intended to major in business. While helping her plan the courses she needed to complete her degree, I pointed out to her that she still needed to take a course in philosophy. After I made this point, here's how our conversation went.

Student (in a somewhat irritated tone): "Why do I have to take philosophy? I'm a business major."

Dr. Cuseo: "Because philosophy is an important component of a liberal arts education."

Student (in a very agitated tone): "I'm not liberal and I don't want to be a liberal. I'm conservative and so are my parents; we all voted for Ronald Reagan last election!"

Many student (and their parents) do not know what the term "liberal arts" truly means.

The student probably would have picked choice "1" as her answer to the multiple-choice question posed at the start of this chapter. (She would have been wrong because option "5" is the correct answer.) Literally translated, the term "liberal arts" derives from the Latin words "liberales"—meaning to *liberate* or *free*, and "artes"—meaning *skills*. Thus, "skills for freedom" is the most accurate meaning of the term "liberal arts."

The roots of the "liberal arts" date back to the origin of modern civilization—to the ancient Greeks and Romans—who advocated for a democratic government in which the people choose (elect) their own leaders. In a democracy or free society, people should be *liberated* from uncritical dependence on a dictator or autocrat. To preserve political freedom and engage effectively in self-governance, citizens in a democracy needed to be well-educated, critical thinkers capable of making wise choices about whom they elect as their leaders and lawmakers (11, 19).

The political ideals of the ancient Greeks and Romans were shared by the founding fathers of the United States who also emphasized the importance of an educated citizenry for preserving America's new democracy. As Thomas Jefferson, third president of the United States, wrote in 1801:

> "I know of no safe depository of the ultimate powers of a society but the people themselves; and if we think them not enlightened enough to exercise control with a wholesome discretion [responsible decision-making], the remedy is not to take power from them, but to inform their discretion by education." (40).

Thus, the origins of liberal arts are rooted in the democratic ideal that education is essential for preserving political freedom. Citizens educated in the liberal arts acquire the breadth of knowledge and depth of thinking needed to vote wisely, preserve democracy, and oppose autocracy (dictatorship). In other words, citizens must learn to think for themselves rather than have someone else (a dictator) do their thinking for them.

The importance of a knowledgeable, critical-thinking citizenry for preserving democracy remains relevant today. Contemporary political campaigns make frequent use of manipulative media advertisements that rely on short sound bites, one-sided arguments, and powerful visual images, which are intentionally designed to appeal to voters' emotions rather than their reasoning skills (65).

Over time, the term "liberal arts" acquired the additional meaning of liberating (freeing) people to be *self-directed* individuals who make choices and decisions guided by their own, well-informed ideas and personal values rather than by blind conformity to the ideas and values of others (162). Self-directed human beings are liberated not only from manipulation and control by political figures, but also from:

- Any authority figure—e.g., they question and challenge excessive use or abuse of authority by parents, teachers, or law enforcers;

- Peers—e.g., they resist irrational or unethical peer pressure; and

- Media—e.g., they detect and reject forms of advertisements designed to manipulate their self-image or material needs.

The Liberal Arts Curriculum

Based on this educational philosophy of the ancient Greeks and Romans, the first liberal arts curriculum (collection of courses) was developed during the Middle Ages and consisted of seven courses divided into two general areas: (a) the trivium (a set of three courses): logic, grammar, and rhetoric—the art of oral argumentation and persuasion, and (b) the quadrivium (a set of four courses): music, arithmetic, geometry, and astronomy (134). The original liberal arts curriculum reflected the belief that individuals who experienced these courses would acquire (a) a *broad* base of knowledge that left them well informed in a variety of different subjects and (b) a complete set of mental skills that enabled them to think *deeply* and *critically*.

The purpose of the original liberal arts curriculum has withstood the test of time. Today's colleges and universities continue to offer a liberal arts curriculum designed to provide students with a broad base of knowledge in multiple subject areas that equips them with critical thinking skills. The liberal arts curriculum today is sometimes called *general education*—to represent the fact that it leads to knowledge and skills that are "general" or flexible, rather than rigid or narrowly specialized. General education signifies what *all* college graduates learn in common—i.e., what every college graduate should know and be able to do, regardless of their specific major or specialized field may be (10). On some campuses, the liberal arts are also referred to as:

1. **The core curriculum:** "Core" standing for what is central or essential for effective performance in any field; or

2. **Breadth requirements:** Referring to the fact that they embrace a wide range of subject areas designed to provide a broad base of knowledge and skills.

Reflection 1.2

To be successful in any major or career, what do you think a person should:

1. Know?
2. Be able to do?

The liberal arts encourage you to be "your own person" and to always ask, "Why?" It is the component of your college education which empowers you to be an independent thinker with an inquiring mind that questions authority and resists conformity.

"Successful first-year students must not only get off to a good start academically and learn how to learn, but they must begin to appreciate what it means to become an educated person."

–Lee Upcraft, John Gardner, and Betsy Barefoot, *Challenging and Supporting the First-Year Student*

Subject Areas (Divisions of Knowledge) in the Liberal Arts Curriculum

On average, about twelve to fourteen courses, or about one-third of a college graduate's course credits, are required general education courses taken from the liberal arts curriculum (39). The subject areas in the contemporary liberal arts curriculum have expanded well beyond the seven courses that comprised the original curriculum at medieval universities. The *divisions* of knowledge that comprise the liberal arts today, and the *courses* that make up each division, vary somewhat from campus to campus. Campuses also vary in terms of the nature and number of required courses within each division of knowledge, as well as the range or variety of course choices that students may choose from to fulfill their general education requirements.

Despite campus-to-campus variation in the number and nature of courses required, the liberal arts curriculum on every campus represents the areas of knowledge and the types of skills that all college graduates should possess. Listed below are the general divisions of knowledge and related subject areas that comprise the liberal arts curriculum on most campuses today. As you read the following divisions of knowledge, highlight any subject areas in which you have never had a course.

Humanities

Courses in this division of the liberal arts curriculum focus on the *human experience* and *human culture*. They ask the "big questions" that arise in the life of all human beings, such as: Why are we here? What is the meaning or purpose of our existence? How should I live? What is the good life? Is there life after death? Courses in this branch of the liberal arts are also designed to develop those skills that relate specifically to human language, such as reading, writing, and speaking.

Primary Subject Areas

- **English composition:** Writing clearly, critically, and persuasively.
- **Speech:** Speaking eloquently and persuasively.
- **Literature:** Reading critically and appreciating the artistic merit of various literary genres (forms of writing), such as novels, short stories, poems, plays, and essays.
- **Foreign languages:** Listening, speaking, reading, and writing in languages other than one's native tongue.
- **Philosophy:** Thinking rationally, developing wisdom (the ability to use knowledge prudently), and living an ethically principled life.
- **Religious studies:** Understanding how humans conceive of and express their faith in a transcendent (supreme) being.
- **History:** Understanding past events, their causes, their influence on current events, and their implications for future events. (**Note:** Some campuses classify history in the social sciences rather than the humanities.)

Fine Arts

Courses in this division of the liberal arts curriculum focus largely on the *artistic expression*, asking such questions as: How do humans create, demonstrate, and appreciate what is beautiful? How do humans express themselves aesthetically (through the senses) with imagination, originality, style, and elegance?

Primary Subject Areas

- **Visual arts:** Creating and appreciating human expression through visual representation (drawing, painting, sculpture, photography, and graphic design).

- **Musical arts:** Appreciating and creating rhythmical arrangements of sounds.

- **Performing arts:** Appreciating and expressing creativity through drama and dance.

Mathematics

Courses in this division of the liberal arts curriculum are designed to promote skills in *numerical* calculation, *quantitative* reasoning, and problem solving.

Primary Subject Areas

- **Algebra:** Mathematical reasoning through symbolic representation of numbers in a language of letters that vary in size or quantity.

- **Statistics:** Mathematical methods for summarizing, estimating probabilities, representing and understanding numerical information depicted in graphs, charts, and tables, and drawing accurate conclusions from quantitative data.

- **Calculus:** Higher mathematical methods for calculating the rate at which the quantity of one entity changes in relation to another and mathematical methods for measuring areas enclosed by curves.

Natural Sciences

Courses in this division of the liberal arts curriculum are devoted to systematic observation of the *physical world* and explanation of *natural phenomena*. They ask such questions as: What causes the physical events that take place in the natural world? How can we predict and control these events? How do we promote a symbiotic relationship between the human world and the natural (physical) environment that serves to sustain the survival of both?

Primary Subject Areas

- **Biology:** Understanding the structure and underlying processes of all living things.

- **Chemistry:** Understanding the composition of natural and synthetic (man-made) substances and how these substances may be changed or developed.

- **Physics:** Understanding the properties of physical matter and the principles of energy, motion, and electrical and magnetic forces.

> "Dancing is silent poetry."
> –Simonides, ancient Greek poet

> "The universe is a grand book which cannot be read until one learns to comprehend the language and become familiar with the characters of which it is composed. It is written in the language of mathematics."
> –Galileo Galilei, a.k.a., Galileo, -seventeenth century Italian physicist, mathematician, astronomer, and philosopher

> "Science is an imaginative adventure of the mind seeking truth in a world of mystery."
> –Sir Cyril Herman Hinshelwood, Nobel Prize-winning English chemist

- **Geology:** Understanding the composition of the earth and the natural processes that have shaped its development.
- **Astronomy:** Understanding the composition and motion of celestial bodies that comprise the universe.

Social and Behavioral Sciences

Courses in this division of the liberal arts curriculum focus on the observation of *human behavior*, both individually and in groups, asking such questions as: What causes humans to behave the way they do? How can we predict, control, or improve human behavior and interpersonal interaction?

Primary Subject Areas

- **Psychology:** Understanding the human mind, its conscious and subconscious processes, and the underlying causes of human behavior.
- **Sociology:** Understanding the structure, interaction, and collective behavior of organized social groups, institutions, or systems that comprise human society (e.g., family, education, religion, criminal justice, and social services).
- **Anthropology:** Understanding the cultural and physical origin, development and distribution of the human species.
- **History:** Understanding past events, their causes, their influence on current events, and their implications for future events. (**Note:** Some campuses classify history in the humanities rather than social sciences.)
- **Political Science:** Understanding how societal authority is organized and how this authority is exerted to govern people, make collective decisions, and maintain social order.
- **Economics:** Understanding how the monetary needs of humans are met through the allocation of limited resources, and how material wealth is produced and distributed.
- **Geography:** Understanding how the place (physical location) where humans live influences their cultural and societal development, and how humans influence and are influenced by their surrounding physical environment.

Physical Education and Wellness

Courses in this division of the liberal arts curriculum focus on the *human body*—how to maintain optimal health and attain peak levels of performance—by asking such questions as: How does the body function most effectively? What can humans do to prevent illness, promote wellness, and improve the physical and mental quality of one's life?

Primary Subject Areas

- **Physical education:** Understanding the role of human exercise for promoting health and peak performance.

"Man, the molecule of society, is the subject of social science."
–Henry Charles Carey, leading -nineteenth century American economist

"To eat is a necessity, but to eat intelligently is an art."
–La Rochefoucauld, -seventeenth century French author

- **Nutrition:** Understanding how the body makes use of food and uses it as nourishment to promote health and generate energy.
- **Sexuality:** Understanding the biological, psychological, and social aspects of sexual relations.
- **Drug education:** Understanding how substances (chemicals) that alter the body and mind affect physical health, mental health, and human performance.

Reflection 1.3

Look back at the liberal arts' subject areas in which you have never had a course, and identify which of these areas strike you as particularly interesting or potentially useful. Provide a brief explanation why.

Most of your liberal arts requirements will be taken during your first two years of college. Don't be surprised or discouraged to find that some of these requirements sound similar to courses you had in high school. Don't begin to think that you will be bored to tears because you know all there is to know about these fields of study. College courses in the same subject areas that you may have experienced in high school will not be videotape replays of what you have already learned. You will move beyond basic competency in these subjects to more advanced levels of proficiency. You will delve more deeply into these subjects, learn about them in greater depth, and think about them at a higher level (39). In fact, research indicates that most of the gains in thinking that students make in college take place during their first two years—the very years in which they are taking most of their liberal arts courses (127).

The breadth of knowledge you acquire in the liberal arts allows you to stand on the shoulders of intellectual giants from a wide range of fields and capitalize on their collective wisdom. Also, keep in mind that the liberal arts do not just enable you to acquire a broad base of knowledge; they also discipline your mind to *think* in a wide variety of ways. This is why different academic subjects are often referred to as *disciplines*—by learning them, you begin to develop the "mental discipline" that faculty in these fields have spent years of their lives developing. For instance, when you study history, algebra, biology, and art, you are disciplining your mind to think chronologically (history), symbolically (algebra), scientifically (biology), and creatively (art). The diverse subjects in different divisions of the liberal arts will promote your mental flexibility by stretching your mind to think in a wide variety of ways, which include thinking:

- In the form of words, numbers, and images,
- In terms of specific parts and whole patterns,
- Locally and globally,
- Concretely and abstractly,
- Systematically (in sequential steps) and intuitively (in sudden leaps),

- Factually and imaginatively, and
- Objectively, subjectively, and symbolically (49, 78).

The Liberal Arts "Liberates" You from Narrowness by Broadening Your Perspective of the World Around You

The liberal arts provide you with a broad base of knowledge by exposing you to diverse fields of study. This breadth of knowledge will widen your perspective on the world around you (26). The key components of this broader perspective are organized and illustrated in the following figure.

In **Figure 1.1**, the center circle represents the self. Fanning out to the right of the self is a series of arches that encompass the **social-spatial perspective**, which includes increasingly larger social groups and more distant places—ranging from the narrowest perspective (the individual)—to the widest perspective (the universe). The liberal arts liberate you from the narrow "tunnel vision" of a self-centered (egocentric) perspective; it provides a panoramic perspective of the world that empowers you to step outside yourself and see yourself in relation to other people and other places.

In **Figure 1.1**, to the left of the self are three arches labeled the *chronological perspective*, which represent the three key dimensions of time: past (historical), present (contemporary), and future (futuristic). The liberal arts not only widen your perspective, they also lengthen it by stretching your vision beyond the present—enabling you to see yourself in relation to humans who have lived before us and who will live after us. The chronological perspective gives you hindsight to see where the world has been, insight into the world's current condition, and foresight to see where the world is going.

It could be said that the chronological perspective provides you with a mental "time machine" that allows you to flash back to the past and flash forward to the future, while the *social-spatial* perspective provides you with a conceptual telescope that enables you to view people and places that are far away. These two broadening perspectives developed by the liberal arts combine to expand your perspective

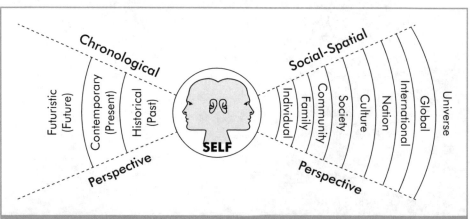

Figure 1.1. Multiple Perspectives Developed by the Liberal Arts.

beyond the here and now, enabling you to view and appreciate the experiences of different people living in different places at different times.

Specific elements that comprise each of these broadening perspectives of the liberal arts are described below.

Elements of the Social-Spatial Perspective: Different Persons and Places

The Perspective of Family

Moving beyond the perspective of yourself as an individual, you are part of a larger social unit—your *family*. Members of your family have undoubtedly influenced the person you are today and how you got to be that way. Moreover, your family has not only influenced you; you have influenced your family. For example, your decision to go to college has likely elevated your family's sense of pride and may influence other family members' decision to attend college. In addition, if or when you have children, your graduation from college will influence their future welfare. As will be mentioned in Chapter 3, children of college graduates experience improved intellectual development, better physical health, and greater economic security (24, 25, 126, 127).

The Perspective of Community

Moving beyond the family, you are also a member of a larger social unit—your *community*. This wider social circle includes friends and neighbors at home, at school, and at work. These are the communities in which you can begin to take action to improve the human condition. If you want to make the world a better place, this is the place to start—through civic engagement in your local communities.

Civic-minded and civically responsible step beyond their narrow self-interests and selflessly share their time or resources to help members of their community, particularly those in need. They demonstrate their humanity by being *humane*—i.e., showing genuine compassion for the humans less fortunate than themselves, and by being *humanitarian*—i.e., engaging in action that promotes the welfare of fellow humans.

The Perspective of Society

Moving beyond your local communities, you are also a member of a larger *society*—a group of people organized under the same social system. Societies include subgroups divided into different regions (e.g., north, south, east, west), different population densities (e.g., urban, suburban, rural), and different socioeconomic classes (e.g., level of income, education, and job status). Within a society, there are typically subgroups that are stratified (layered) into different social classes with unequal levels of economic resources. For example, in the United States, the wealthiest 20 percent of the American population controls approximately 50 percent of the total American income, while the 20 percent of Americans with the lowest level of income controls only 4 percent of the nation's wealth (154). Groups occupying

"*Think globally, act locally.*"

–Patrick Geddes, Scottish urban planner and social activist

lower socioeconomic strata have fewer social and economic resources, and fewer educational and occupational opportunities (57).

Reflection 1.4

What do you think is the primary reason poverty exists in human societies? Do you believe that it has the potential to be eliminated? If so, what do you see as the key to its elimination? Or, do you see is it an inevitable element of life in human societies? If so, why?

The Perspective of Culture

Culture can be broadly defined as a distinctive pattern of beliefs and values that are learned by a group of people who share the same social heritage and traditions. In short, culture is the whole way in which a group of people has learned to live; it includes their customary style of speaking (language), fashion, food, art, music, values, and beliefs.

It could be said that the academic divisions of knowledge that comprise the liberal arts curriculum represent different components of human culture that scholars have decided to specialize in and study carefully. Thus, by becoming knowledgeable in these different fields, you become "cultured" or a person "of culture." **Box 1.1** is a summary of key components of culture that a group may share. Notice how these cultural components correspond to the major divisions of knowledge and fields of study in the liberal arts.

BOX 1.1   Key Components of Culture

- **Linguistic** (Language): How group members communicate through written or spoken word, and through nonverbal communication (body language).

- **Political:** How the group organizes societal authority and uses it to govern itself, make collective decisions, and maintain social order.

- **Economic:** How the material wants and needs of the group are met through the allocation of limited resources, and how wealth is distributed among its members.

- **Geographic:** How the group's physical location influences the nature of their social interactions and affects the way the group adapts to and uses their environment.

- **Aesthetic:** How the group appreciates and expresses artistic beauty and creativity through the fine arts (e.g., visual art, music, theater, literature, and dance).

- **Scientific:** How the group views, understands, and investigates natural phenomena through systematic research (e.g., scientific tests and experiments).

- **Ecological:** How the group views the interrelationship between the biological world (human beings and other living creatures) and the natural world (surrounding physical environment).

- **Anthropological:** How the group's culture originated, evolved, and developed over time.
- **Sociological:** How the group's society is structured or organized into social subgroups and social institutions.
- **Psychological:** How its group members tend to think, feel, and interact; and how their attitudes, opinions, or beliefs have been acquired.
- **Philosophical:** The group's ideas or views on wisdom, goodness, truth, and the meaning or purpose of life.
- **Theological:** The group's conception of, and beliefs about a transcendent, supreme being, and how its members express their shared faith in a supreme being.

Sometimes, the terms "culture" and "society" are used interchangeably as if they were synonymous terms; however, they each refer to a different aspect of humanity. Society is a group of people organized under the same social system. For example, all members of American society are organized under the same system of government, justice, and education. In contrast, culture is what members of a certain group of people actually have in common with respect to their past traditions and current ways of living, regardless of the particular society or social system in which they live (117). For example, cultural differences can exist within the same society, resulting in a "multicultural" society.

A group of people who share the same culture is referred to as an *ethnic group*. Thus, an ethnic group refers to a group of people *who* share the same culture, and culture refers to *what* that ethnic group shares in common. An ethnic group's common cultural characteristics are the result of *socialization*—i.e., they are *learned* and passed on through group members' shared social environment and experiences; they not inherited or transmitted genetically. (Note how the environmental nature of culture is consistent with related terms such as growing living organisms in a "culture" or "cultivating" crops.)

The National Perspective

Beyond being a member of society, you are also a citizen of a nation. In a democratic nation, citizens are expected to participate in its governance system—as voters, and in its judicial system—as jurors. It is noteworthy that American citizens between the ages of eighteen and twenty-four have displayed the lowest voter-turnout rate of any age group that is eligible to vote (45). If you are a student in this age group, we strongly encourage you to become an engaged citizen and participate in the voting process. The right to vote is the hallmark of a democratic nation, and having the privilege of being a citizen in a free nation brings with it the responsibility of participating in your country's governance through the voting process.

Remember: the original purpose of the liberal arts (and a college education) was to educate citizens broadly and deeply, so they could vote wisely.

The International Perspective

Moving beyond your particular country of citizenship, you are also a member of an international world that includes close to two hundred nations (137). The life of citizens in all nations today is affected by events that cross national borders; boundaries between nations are blurring and breaking down as a result of increased international travel, international trading, and multinational corporations. Furthermore, communication and interaction among citizens of different nations is greater today than at any other time in world history—due in large part to rapid advances in electronic technology (50, 145). The worldwide Web (www) has made today's world a "small world after all" and success in it requires an international perspective.

By learning from and about different nations, you become much more than a citizen of your own country, you become cosmopolitan—a citizen of the world.

The Global Perspective

Broader than an international perspective is the *global* perspective. It includes and unites all members of the human species (almost seven billion and still growing) from all cultures and nation. Despite differences that exist among human groups in terms of their cultural and national experiences, these differences grow from the same soil—they are all rooted in the common ground of our shared humanity.

A global perspective also includes all forms of life inhabiting planet earth and the relationships between these diverse life forms and the earth's natural resources (minerals, air, and water). Humans must remain mindful that they share the earth and its natural resources with approximately 10 million animal species (107) and more than 300,0000 forms of vegetative life (84). As "global citizens" inhabiting the same planet, we have an environmental responsibility to address global issues (e.g., global warming and environmental sustainability), which require striking a healthy balance between making industrial-technological progress, preserving "Mother Earth's" natural resources, and protecting other forms of life that share our planet.

Perspective of the Universe (Cosmos)

Beyond the global perspective is the broadest of all perspectives—the *universe*. Just as we should guard against being ethnocentric—thinking that our culture is the center of humanity, we should also guard against being geocentric—thinking that our planet is the center of the universe. All heavenly bodies do not revolve around planet earth. The sun doesn't rise in the east and set in the west; our planet rotates around the sun to produce our earthly experiences of day and night.

"Get involved. Don't gripe about things unless you are making an effort to change them. You can make a difference if you dare."

–Richard C. Holbrooke, former director of the Peace Corps and American ambassador to the United Nations

"A liberal [arts] education frees a person from the prison-house of class, race, time, place, background, family, and nation."

–Robert Hutchins, former dean of Yale Law School and president of the University of Chicago

"Treat the Earth well. It was not given to you by your parents. It was loaned to you by your children."

–Kenyan proverb

"In astronomy, you must get used to viewing the earth as just one planet in the larger context of the universe."

–Physics professor (quoted in Donald, 2002)

Astronauts who have traveled beyond the earth's force of gravity and viewed the universe from the perspective of outer space often describe their expanded perspective as a "spiritual" experience; and some scholars contend that exploring the universe mentally by reflecting on its massive and mysterious nature, how it may have begun, where it may be going, and whether it will ever end are spiritual questions (165). Whether you view the universe through the physical telescope of astronomy or the spiritual scope of reflective contemplation, it qualifies as the broadest of all social-spatial perspectives developed by the liberal arts.

In sum, the broadening social-spatial perspectives of the liberal arts expand your perception and appreciation of different people and different places. At the same time, they combat the seven types of narrow, close-minded perspectives described in **Box 1.2**.

BOX 1.2   Seven Narrow Viewpoints Combated by the Broadening Perspectives of the Liberal Arts

1. **Egocentrism:** Viewing oneself as the center of all things.

2. **Parochialism** (a.k.a., *provincialism*)**:** Narrow-mindedness and unwillingness to expand one's viewpoints beyond a local perspective.

3. **Regionalism:** Centering on one's own geographical region and favoring everything related to it.

4. **Ethnocentrism:** Belief that one's own cultural customs and values are superior to all others.

5. **Nationalism:** Belief that the interests, needs, or wants of one's own nation should be placed ahead of all other nations.

6. **Anthropocentrism:** Belief that humans are the center of the world and their needs or wants take precedence over all other life forms and planetary resources.

7. **Geocentrism:** Viewing planet Earth as the center of the universe.

Reflection 1.5

Look back at the seven narrow viewpoints combated by the liberal arts. For each perspective, think of a college course you could take that develops this perspective. If you are unsure about what courses are designed to develop any of these perspectives, take a look at the course descriptions in your college catalogue or bulletin (either in print or online).

◆ Elements of the Chronological Perspective: The Perspective of Different Times

In addition to expanding your perspective of the word to include other people and places, the liberal arts also stretches your perspective of time to include the past, present, and future.

Historical Perspective

A *historical* perspective is critical for understanding the root causes of the current human condition and world situation. The humanity in the world today is a collective product of social and natural history. Don't forget that our earth is estimated to be more than 4.5 billion years old and our human ancestors date back more than 250,000 years (84). Thus, our current lives represent a very small frame of time in a very long chronological reel. Every human advancement and convenience we enjoy today reflects the collective effort and cumulative knowledge of diverse human groups that has unfolded over thousands of years of history.

By studying the past, we can build on our ancestors' achievements and learn from their mistakes. For example, by understanding the causes and consequences of the holocaust, we can reduce the risk that an atrocious "crime against humanity" of such size and scope will ever happen again.

Contemporary Perspective

The *contemporary* perspective focuses on understanding the current world situation and the events that comprise today's news. One major goal of a liberal arts education is to increase your understanding the contemporary human condition so that you may have the wisdom to improve it (103). For example, a contemporary perspective will enable you to see that despite historical progress in our nation's acceptance and appreciation of different ethnic and racial groups, the Unites States currently remains a nation deeply divided with respect to differences in culture, religion, and social class (29).

Futuristic Perspective

The *futuristic* perspective allows you to flash forward and envision what the world will be like years from now. This perspective focuses on such questions as: Will you leave the world a better or worse place for humans who will inhabit after your departure, including our children and grandchildren? How can humans living today move beyond short-term, shortsighted thinking and adopt a long-range vision that anticipates the consequences of their current actions on future generations of humans?

To sum up, a comprehensive chronological perspective brings the past, present, and future into focus on a single screen. It enables us to see how the current world is a short segment of a long temporal sequence that has been shaped by previous events and will shape future events.

In light of the information you have read in this chapter, how would you interpret the following statement: "We can't know where we're going until we know where we've been?"

The Synoptic Perspective: Integrating Diverse Perspectives to Form a Unified Whole

The liberal arts not only help you appreciate multiple perspectives; they help you *integrate* them into a meaningful whole (82). Understanding how the perspectives of time, place, and person interrelate to form a unified whole is sometimes referred to as a *synoptic* perspective (43, 70). The word derives from a combination of two different roots: "syn"—meaning "together" (as in the word "synthesize"), and "optic"—meaning "to see." Thus, a *synoptic* perspective literally means to "see things together" or "see the whole." It enables you to see how all the trees come together to form the forest.

By seeing yourself as an integral part of humankind, you become integrated with the whole of humanity; you're able to see how you, as an individual, fit into the "big picture"—the larger scheme of things (69). When we view ourselves as nested within a web of interconnections with other places, people, and times (as shown in **Figures 1.2 and 1.3**), we become aware of the common humanity we all share with all living humans and all humans who have ever lived.

Developing an increased sense of connection with humankind serves to decrease feelings of personal isolation or alienation (18). In his book *The Perfect Education* Kenneth Eble skillfully describes this benefit of a liberal arts education:

> The expanded perspectives on time, place, and people developed by the liberal arts serve to widen, lengthen, and deepen your thinking. You are liberated from thinking in terms of the here and now, and you are empowered to view the world from "long ago and far away."

It can provide that over-arching life of a people, a community, a world that was going on before the individual came onto the scene and that will continue on after [s]he departs. By such means we come to see the world not alone. Our joys are more intense for being shared. Our sorrows are less destructive for our knowing universal sorrow. Our fears of death fade before the commonness of the occurrence (52).

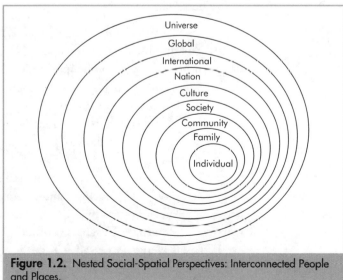

Figure 1.2. Nested Social-Spatial Perspectives: Interconnected People and Places.

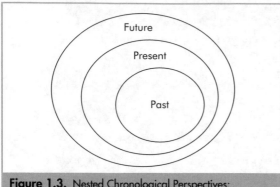

Figure 1.3. Nested Chronological Perspectives: Interconnected Times.

Liberating the Development of the "Whole Person"

One of the most frequently cited goals of experiencing the liberal arts is to "know thyself" (44). In addition to expanding your knowledge of the outer world, they expand knowledge of your inner self. To truly know thyself—to be become fully self-aware—you must know your *whole* self. The liberal arts do this by liberating you from another form of narrowness—a narrow, single-dimensional view of yourself—expanding awareness of the multiplicity of dimensions that comprise the "self." As illustrated in **Figure 1.4**, the human self is comprised of diverse dimensions that join together to form the "whole person."

Key Dimensions of the Self

- **Intellectual:** Your knowledge, perspectives, and ways of thinking,
- **Emotional:** Your feelings, self-esteem, emotional intelligence, and mental health,
- **Social:** Your interpersonal interactions and relationships,
- **Physical:** Your bodily health and wellness,
- **Vocational:** Your occupational (career) development and satisfaction,
- **Ethical:** Your values, character, and moral convictions,
- **Spiritual:** Your beliefs about the meaning or purpose of life and the hereafter,
- **Personal:** Your identity, self-concept, and capacity for self-management.

Each of the above elements of self plays an influential role in promoting a human being's health, success, and happiness. Research strongly suggests that the quality of an individual's life depends on attention to and development of all key elements of the self. For instance, it has been found that people who are healthy (physically and mentally) and successful (personally and professionally) attend to and integrate different dimensions of their self, enabling them to lead well-rounded and well-balanced lives (41, 66, 70).

One of the primary goals of the liberal arts is to provide a "well-rounded" education that promotes, develops, and integrates the whole person (87). Research on college students confirms that their college experience affects them in multiple ways and develops multiple dimensions of self (25, 58, 126).

Different elements of self will be discussed separately in this chapter to keep them clear in your mind. However, in reality, they do not operate independently; they are interconnected and influence one another. (This is why the elements of the self in **Figure 1.4** are depicted as links in an interconnected chain.) The self is a diverse, multidimensional entity that has the capacity to develop along a variety of interdependent dimensions (97).

Since wholeness is essential for wellness, success and happiness, take the time to carefully read the following descriptions and specific skills associated with each of the eight elements of holistic development. As you are read the specific skills and qualities listed beneath each of the eight elements, place a checkmark beside any skill that is particularly important to you. You may check more than one skill in each area.

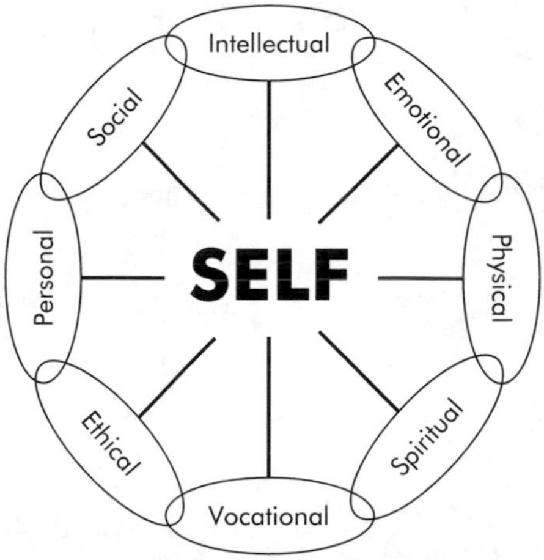

Figure 1.4. Key Elements of Holistic (Whole-Person) Development.

Skills and Qualities Associated with Each Element of Holistic (Whole-Person) Development

Intellectual Development: Acquiring knowledge, learning how to learn deeply and to think at a higher level.

Specific Goals and Skills:

- Becoming aware of your intellectual abilities, interests, and learning styles.
- Maintaining attention and concentration.
- Improving your ability to retain knowledge (long-term memory).
- Moving beyond memorization to higher levels of thinking.
- Acquiring effective research skills for accessing information from a variety of sources and systems.
- Viewing issues from multiple angles or viewpoints (psychological, social, political, economic, etc.) in order to attain a balanced, comprehensive perspective.
- Critically evaluating ideas in terms of their truth and value.
- Thinking creatively or imaginatively.
- Responding constructively to differing viewpoints or opposing arguments.
- Detecting and rejecting persuasion tactics that appeal to emotions rather than reason.

Emotional Development: Strengthening your ability to understand, control, and express emotions.

Specific Goals and Skills:

- Dealing with personal emotions in an honest, non-defensive manner.
- Maintaining a healthy balance between emotional control and emotional expression.

STUDENT PERSPECTIVE

"Being successful is being balanced in every aspect of your life."

–First-year college student, in response to the question: "What does being successful mean to you?"

"

"Integration of learning is the ability to connect information from disparate contexts and perspectives—for example, to connect one field of study with another, the past with the present, one part with the whole—and vice versa."

–Wabash National Study of Liberal Arts Education (2007)

- Responding with empathy and sensitivity to emotions experienced by others.
- Dealing effectively with depression.
- Dealing effectively with anger.
- Using effective stress-management strategies to control anxiety and tension.
- Responding effectively to frustrations and setbacks.
- Dealing effectively with fear of failure and poor performance.
- Accepting feedback in a constructive, non-defensive manner.
- Maintaining optimism and enthusiasm.

Social Development: Enhancing the quality and depth of your interpersonal relationships.

Specific Goals and Skills:

- Developing effective conversational skills.
- Becoming an effective listener.
- Relating effectively to others in one-to-one, small-group, and large-group situations.
- Collaborating effectively with others when working in groups or teams.
- Overcoming shyness.
- Developing more meaningful and intimate relationships.
- Dealing with interpersonal conflicts assertively, rather than aggressively or passively.
- Providing feedback to others in a constructive and considerate manner.
- Relating effectively with others from different cultural backgrounds and lifestyles.
- Developing leadership skills.

Ethical Development: Developing a clear value system for guiding life choices and decisions; building moral character—the ability to make and act on ethical judgments, and to demonstrate consistency between convictions (beliefs) and commitments (actions).

Specific Goals and Skills:

- Gaining deeper self-awareness of your values and ethical assumptions.
- Making personal choices and life decisions based on a meaningful value system.
- Developing the capacity to think and act with personal integrity and authenticity.
- Using electronic technology in an ethical and civil manner.
- Resisting social pressure to act in ways that are inconsistent with your values.
- Treating others in an ethical or morally responsible manner.

- Exercising individual freedom without infringing on the rights of others.
- Developing concern and commitment for human rights and social justice.
- Developing the courage to challenge or confront others who violate human rights and social justice.
- Becoming an ethically responsible citizen.

Physical Development: Applying knowledge about the human body to prevent disease, preserve wellness, and promote peak performance.

Specific Goals and Skills:

- Developing awareness of your physical condition and state of health.
- Applying knowledge about exercise and fitness training to improve your physical and mental health.
- Understanding how sleep patterns affect health and performance.
- Maintaining a healthy balance between work, recreation, and relaxation.
- Acquiring knowledge about nutrition to reduce risk of illness and promote peak performance.
- Gaining knowledge about nutritional imbalances and eating disorders.
- Developing a positive body image.
- Becoming aware of the effects of drugs and their impact on physical and mental well-being.
- Acquiring knowledge about human sexuality, sexual relations, and sexually transmitted diseases.
- Understanding how biological differences affect male-female relationships and gender orientation.

Spiritual Development: Searching for answers to the "big questions," such as the meaning or purpose of life and death, and exploring issues that transcend human life and the physical or material world.

Specific Goals and Skills:

- Developing a philosophy of life or world view about the meaning and purpose of human existence.
- Exploring the unknown or what cannot be completely understood scientifically.
- Exploring the mysteries associated with the origin of the universe.
- Searching for the connection between the self and the larger world or cosmos.
- Searching for the mystical or supernatural—that which transcends the boundaries of the natural world.
- Being open to examining questions relating to death and life after death.
- Being open to examining questions about the possible existence of a supreme being or higher power.

> " Chi rispetta sara rippetato.
> (Respect others and you will be respected.)
> –Italian proverb

> "The moral challenge is simply to abide by the knowledge we already have."
> —Soren Kierkegaard, nineteenth century Danish philosopher and theologian

> "If you don't stand for something you will fall for anything."
> –Malcolm X, African-American Muslim minister, public speaker, and human rights activist

> "A man too busy to take care of his health is like a mechanic too busy to take care of his tools."
> –Spanish proverb

"Everyone is a house with four rooms: a physical, a mental, an emotional, and a spiritual. Most of us tend to live in one room most of the time but unless we go into every room every day, even if only to keep it aired, we are not complete."

—Native American proverb

"Remember, no one can make you feel inferior without your consent."

–Eleanor Roosevelt, human rights activities, author, and diplomat

- Acquiring knowledge about different approaches to spirituality and their underlying beliefs or assumptions.
- Understanding the difference and relationship between faith and reason.
- Becoming aware and tolerant of religious beliefs and practices.

Vocational Development: Exploring occupational options, making career choices wisely, and developing skills needed for lifelong career success.

Specific Goals and Skills:

- Understanding the relationship between college majors and careers.
- Using effective strategies for exploring and identifying potential careers.
- Identifying career options that are compatible with your personal values, interests, and talents.
- Acquiring work experience in fields that relate to your career interests.
- Developing an effective resumé and portfolio.
- Adopting effective strategies for identifying personal references and sources for letters of recommendation.
- Acquiring effective job search strategies.
- Using effective strategies for writing letters of inquiry and application to potential employers.
- Developing strategies for performing successfully in personal interviews.
- Acquiring networking skills for connecting with potential employers.

Personal Development: Developing positive self-beliefs, attitudes, and habits.

Specific Goals and Skills:

- Developing a strong sense of personal identity and a coherent self-concept. (Who am I?)
- Finding a sense of purpose and direction in life. (Who will I become?)
- Developing self-respect and self-esteem.
- Increasing self-confidence.
- Developing self-efficacy—belief that the outcomes of one's life can be controlled by your own initiative and effort.
- Setting realistic personal goals and priorities.
- Becoming self-motivated and self-disciplined.
- Developing the persistence and perseverance to reach long-range personal goals.
- Acquiring practical skills for managing personal resources (e.g. time and money) effectively and efficiently.
- Becoming independent, self-directed, and self-reliant.

The Co-Curriculum: Out-of-Class Learning Experiences

The impact of the liberal arts is magnified when you take advantage of the total college environment. This includes not only courses in the curriculum, but also learning experiences outside the classroom—referred to as the *co-curriculum*. Co-curricular experiences include educational discussions you have with your peers and professors outside the classroom, as well as your participation in the variety of events and programs offered on your campus. Research strongly suggests out-of-class learning experiences as being equally important to your overall development as the course curriculum (85, 86); hence, they are referred to as *co*-curricular (not extracurricular) experiences. Studies show that students who become actively involved with the co-curriculum are more likely to:

- Enjoy their college experience;
- Graduate from college; and
- Develop leadership skills that they continue to use beyond college (12).

The learning that takes place in college courses is primarily vicarious—that is, you learn from or through somebody else (e.g., by listening to professors in class and by reading outside of class). While this type of academic learning is valuable, it needs to be complemented and augmented by *experiential* learning—i.e., learning directly through first-hand experiences. For example, leadership cannot be developed solely by listening to lectures and reading books about leadership. In order to fully develop your leadership skills, you need to have leadership *experiences*, such as those developed by "leading a [discussion] group in class, holding office in student government or by being captain of a sports team" (10). College graduates who participated in co-curricular experiences involving leadership while in college consistently report that these experiences allowed them to develop skills that enhanced their job performance and career advancement. College graduates' reports are confirmed by on-the-job evaluations of college alumni, which indicate that co-curricular involvement during college, particularly if it involved leadership experience, is the best predictor of successful

"Students may be pushed into careers by their families, while others have picked one just to relieve their anxiety about not having a career choice. Still others may have picked popular or lucrative careers, knowing nothing of what they're really like or what it takes to prepare for them."

—Lee Upcraft, Joni Finney, and Peter Garland, student development specialists

"I'm a great believer in luck and I find the harder I work, the more I have of it."

–Thomas Jefferson, third president of the United States, and founder of the University of Virginia

managerial performance. Furthermore, students' co-curricular leadership experiences in college are more strongly associated with the managerial success of college graduates than the prestige of the college they attended (126, 127).

PERSONAL EXPERIENCE | Aaron Thompson

I consider myself to be a leader and try to lead by example in both my personal and professional life. Although we all have our preferred styles of leadership, a truly effective leader must be able to adapt his or her style to the specific situation and people at hand. The best way to learn how to do this is by acquiring leadership experiences in multiple situations, both inside and outside the classroom. I have found that effective leadership emerges from exposure to a variety of subject areas and ways of learning, including academic ("book learning") and experiential ("hands on" learning). My course work in the liberal arts and my leadership experiences in campus organizations taught me how to understand others, adapt my leadership style to their cultural background, and to appreciate the multiple factors (e.g., personal, social, and global) that are involved in making positive change happen—which is what leadership is all about. The general education you acquire through the liberal arts curriculum and co-curricular experiences will combine to provide you with the broad perspectives and cross-situational skills needed to be an effective leader.

Listed in **Box 1.3** below are some of the key programs and services that comprise the co-curriculum accompanied by the primary dimension of the self that they are designed to develop. As you read through the list, note any area(s) in which you think you have leadership potential.

General education includes both the curriculum *and* co-curriculum; it involves strategic use of the *total* college environment, both inside and outside the classroom. Take full advantage of your whole college to develop yourself as a whole person.

BOX 1.3   Co-Curricular Programs and Services Promoting Different Dimensions of Holistic Development

Intellectual Development

Academic advising
Learning centers
Library
Tutoring services
Information technology services
Campus speakers
Concerts, theatre productions, art shows

Social and Emotional Development

Student activities
Student clubs and organizations
Counseling services

Spiritual Development

College chaplain
Campus ministry
Peer ministry

Ethical Development

Judicial review board
Student government
Integrity committees and task forces

Vocational Development

Career development services
Internships programs
Service-learning experiences

Vocational Development (continued)

Peer counseling
Peer mentoring
Residential life programs
Commuter programs

Physical Development

Student health services
Wellness programs

Campus athletic activities and intramural sports
Work-study programs
Major and career fairs

Personal Development

Financial aid services
Campus workshops on self-management (e.g., managing time or money)

"General education reform will go beyond questions of content and formal curriculum, important as they are; its goal will be to create an entire college culture that supports the purposes of general education, within the curriculum and beyond."

–Jerry Gaff, author, The Second Wave of General Education Reform

Note: This list represents just a sample of the total number of programs and services that may be available on your campus. As you can see from the list's length, colleges and universities are organized to promote your development in multiple ways. The power of the liberal arts is multiplied when you combine coursework and co-curricular experiences to create a college experience that addresses all key elements of your self.

Reflection 1.8

In what area(s) of holistic development mentioned in the above list do you think you have leadership potential? Why?

"To educate liberally, learning experiences must be offered which facilitate maturity of the whole person. These are goals of student development and clearly they are consistent with the mission and goals of liberal education."

–Theodore Berg, author, Student Development and Liberal Education

Taking Action: Developing a General Education Plan for Making the Most of the Liberal Arts

Since the liberal arts represent a critical component of your college education, it is a component that should be intentionally planned. Advanced educational planning will put you in a position to maximize the impact of the liberal arts on your personal development and career success.

The first step in this planning process is to become familiar with the general education requirements on your campus. You are likely to find these requirements to be organized into general divisions of knowledge (e.g., humanities, fine arts, natural sciences, behavioral sciences). Within each division, there will be specific courses listed that fulfill the general education requirement(s) for that particular division. In some cases, you will have no choice about the courses you must take to fulfill the division's general education requirements; however, in most cases, you will be free

By connecting the curriculum and co-curriculum, general education launches you on a journey toward two forms of "wholeness": (a) an *inner* wholeness in which different elements of your *self* become connected to form a *whole person,* and (b) an *outer* wholeness that connects your self with the *whole world.* This inner and outer quest for wholeness will lead you to a richer, more fulfilling life that is filled with greater breadth and balance.

See Exercise 1.1 at the end of this chapter for step-by-step strategies for developing a general education plan that makes the most of the liberal arts.

Enjoy the greater academic freedom you have in college—and employ it to your advantage—use it strategically to make the most of your college experience and college degree.

to choose from a group of courses. You can use this freedom to develop a general education plan that intentionally develops all of the "liberating" perspectives of a liberal arts education that have been discussed in this chapter.

If you are uncertain about your college major, use your choices for fulfilling general education requirements to test your interests and abilities in fields that you might consider as a major. For example, your campus may have a general education requirement in social or behavioral sciences that requires you to take two courses in this field, but allows you to choose those two courses from a menu of multiple courses in the field—such as anthropology, economics, political science, psychology, or sociology. If you would consider one of these fields as a possible major, take an introductory course in this subject to test your interest and aptitude for it and, while at the same time, fulfill a general education requirement you needed for graduation. This strategy will allow you to use general education as the main highway to progress toward your final destination (a college degree), while simultaneously allowing you to explore potential majors along the way.

Choose your "free" elective courses strategically to strengthen your liberal arts education. Compared to your previous schooling, the college curriculum will provide you with a broader range of courses to choose from, more freedom of choice, and greater academic decision-making opportunities. Electives are college courses that you elect or choose to take. They come in two forms: restricted electives and free electives. *Restricted* electives are courses that you must take, but they are restricted to a list of possible courses that have been specified by your college as fulfilling a requirement in general education or a requirement in your college major.

Free electives are not required for general education or your college major, but they are needed to enable you to accumulate the total number of college credits for a baccalaureate (bachelor's) degree. Free electives give you complete academic freedom to choose any course in the college catalog. (See **Figure 1.5** for a visual map of how your college education includes courses break out into three key categories: general education courses, major courses, and electives.)

Reflection 1.9

Take a look at **Figure 1.5**, the timeline for completing a bachelor's degree is four years. However, the majority of college students today take five years or longer to complete their degree. What do you think accounts for the fact that most college students do not graduate in four years? Do you think you will graduate in four years? Why?

_____

_____

_____

_____

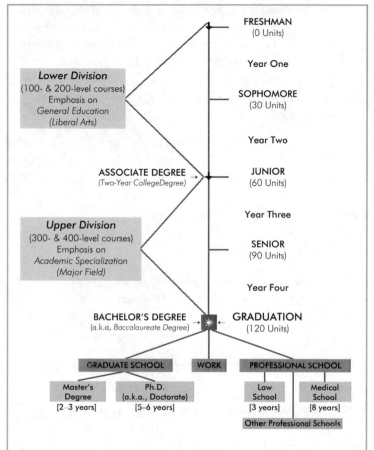

FRESHMAN
(0 Units)

Year One

Lower Division
(100- & 200-level courses)
Emphasis on
General Education
(Liberal Arts)

SOPHOMORE
(30 Units)

Year Two

ASSOCIATE DEGREE →
(Two-Year CollegeDegree)

JUNIOR
(60 Units)

Year Three

Upper Division
(300- & 400-level courses)
Emphasis on
Academic Specialization
(Major Field)

SENIOR
(90 Units)

Year Four

BACHELOR'S DEGREE
(a.k.a, *Baccalaureate Degree*)

GRADUATION
(120 Units)

GRADUATE SCHOOL

WORK

PROFESSIONAL SCHOOL

Master's
Degree
[2–3 years]

Ph.D.
(a.k.a., Doctorate)
[5–6 years]

Law
School
[3 years]

Medical
School
[8 years]

Other Professional Schools

Notes

1. The total number of *general education* units and the total number of units needed to **graduate** with a bachelor's degree may vary somewhat from school to school. Also, the total number of units required for a *major* will vary somewhat from major to major and from school to school.

2. The word "freshman" originated in England in 1596, when every college student was a "fresh" (new) "man." Today, the term "freshman is frequently being replaced by "first-year student" because this a more gender-neutral term.

3. The term "baccalaureate" derives from "Bacchus"—the Greed god of wine and festive celebration, and "laurel"—a wreath made from the laurel plant that ancient Greeks draped around the neek of Olympic champions.

4. It often takes college students longer than four years to graduate due to a variety of reasons, such as working part-time and taking fewer courses per term, needing to repeat courses that were failed or dropped, or making a late change to a different major and needing to fulfill additional requirements for the new major.

5. *Graduate* and *professional* schools are options for continuing to higher levels of education after completion of an undergraduate (college) education.

6. Students going to graduate school on a full-time bassis can sometimes support themselves financially by working part-time as a *teaching assistant* (TA) or *research assistant* (RA). It is also possible to enroll in some graduate or professional school programs on a *part-time* basis, while holding a full-time job.

7. The term "Ph.D." refers to *"Doctor of Philosophy,"* respecting the fact that the first scholars were the ancient Greek *philosophers* (e.g., Socrates, Plato, and Aristotle). However, a Ph.D. can be earned in many different academic fields (Mathematics, Music, Economic, etc.)

8. Compared to graduate school, *professional* school involves advanced education in more "applied" professions (e.g., pharmacy or public administration).

Figure 1.5. A Snapshot of the College Experience and Beyond.

Your curricular experience is likely to be different than that of any other student because the decisions you make about your elective courses over the course of four academic years is likely to result in a final transcript of courses that is identical to no other graduate. With this freedom of choice comes the responsibility of strategic educational planning and decision-making.

The following suggestions are offered as guidelines for using your free electives in a way that magnifies the power of the liberal arts component of your college education.

Take electives that develop *transferable* and durable learning skills, which you can use to promote success throughout your college years and beyond. In addition to taking courses that fulfill general education requirements, you can take elective courses in the liberal arts to further strengthen your repertoire of transferable lifelong skills—such as thinking (e.g., a course in logic or critical thinking), writing (e.g., a course in creative writing), and speaking (e.g., a course in argumentation and debate).

If possible, include *interdisciplinary* courses in your educational plan. Academic disciplines represent a division of labor among scholars in which knowledge is carved up into separate, specialized areas. Deeper and more meaningful learning occurs when bridges are built across these separated and often isolated islands of knowledge. Always be on the lookout to make connections across different courses and be ready to combine the knowledge you acquire from different disciplines to get a more complete understanding of yourself and the world around you.

To help you make cross-disciplinary connections, your college offers some courses that are specifically designed to help you to integrate two or more academic disciplines, which are referred to as *interdisciplinary* courses. For example, psychobiology is an interdisciplinary course that integrates the fields of psychology (focus on the mind) and biology (focus on the body), combining the two in a way that enables you to understand how the mind influences the body and vice versa. Making connections across different subjects not only provides you with a more complete and balanced understanding of the topic. It is also likely that you will find interdisciplinary courses to be a stimulating educational experience. Research indicates that students who participate in interdisciplinary courses report greater gains in learning *and* greater satisfaction with the learning experience (12, 148).

PERSONAL EXPERIENCE | Joe Cuseo

After my first five years of being a college professor in psychology, I came to realize that the most important issues in the world and the issues that mattered most to students were those that extended beyond the boundaries of a single academic field or discipline. Almost every time I mentioned something in one of my psychology courses that happened to relate to an idea that my students were discussing in another course, they would perk up and excitedly point out

(continued)

(or blurt out): "We were just talking about this in _____ (some other) class!" I wasn't sure if I should feel thrilled or depressed when students reported these connections. On the one hand, I was happy that they were seeing the connection and were excited about it; however, on the other hand, the amount of sheer surprise and exhilaration they displayed whenever they saw a connection suggested to me that these connections were a very rare occurrence!

As a result of these observations, I tried to make a more conscious attempt to connect material in my psychology courses with ideas covered in other subject areas. I found that making these connections further increased student interest in the topics I covered in my psychology courses. I became so interested in the idea of making connections between my field and other fields of study that I took a new teaching position at a college which emphasized interdisciplinary, team-taught courses. I went on to team-teach interdisciplinary courses such as: Humor and the Comic Spirit (combining psychology, literature, and film), Sports in American Society (psychology, sociology, and philosophy), Drug Use and Abuse (psychology and criminal justice), and Mind, Brain, and Behavior (psychology and biology). These courses proved to be among my most effective and enjoyable teaching experiences. The students were excited about taking them and making connections across different fields, and the instructors learned a lot from each other. If you have the opportunity to take an interdisciplinary course or participate in an interdisciplinary program, take advantage of it; you should find it to be both a unique and stimulating learning experience.

Your campus may also offer interdisciplinary senior seminars or "capstone courses" designed to integrate general education with your specialized major (47). If such a course is available on your campus, strongly consider taking it. Such senior-level interdisciplinary courses can "tie it altogether" and cultivate the synoptic perspective described in this chapter (p. 15), enabling you to see how different disciplinary perspectives come together to form the "big picture."

Enroll in *service-learning* courses designed to connect learning in the classroom with volunteer service in the community. For example, a sociology course may include assignments involving volunteer service in the local community that you reflect on, and relate to course material through writing assignments or class discussions. Research indicates that students who participate in service-learning courses experience strong gains in multiple areas of self-development, including critical thinking and leadership (13, 147).

Consider pursuing a college *minor* in a liberal arts field that will complement and broaden your major. Most colleges allow you the option of completing a minor along with your major. A college minor usually requires about one-half the number of credits (units) that are required for a college major. Taking a cluster of courses in a field outside your major can be an effective way to strengthen your resume and promote

"Declaring a liberal arts major is not the same as taking a vow of poverty."
—Kent Lehnof, English professor, Chapman University (102)

Employer's Perspective

"A solid foundation in the liberal arts and sciences is necessary for those who want to be corporate leaders."
—George C. Nolen, president and CEO, Siemens Corporation, New York (quoted in AACU, 2007)

Employer's Perspective

"Give me a history major who has done internships and a business major who hasn't, and I'll hire the history major every time."
—William Adrery, senior vice president, Investor Communications Company (quoted in *The New York Times*)

your employment prospects; it demonstrates your versatility and allows you to acquire knowledge and skills that may be underemphasized in your major. For instance, students majoring in such fields as business or computer science may take a cluster of courses in fine arts or humanities to develop skills and perspectives that are not strongly emphasized in their own major field (e.g., a foreign language or international studies course to enhance their career prospects in today's global economy).

If you have interest and talent in a liberal arts field, consider pursuing it as a college *major.* A commonly held myth is that all you can do with a major in a liberal arts field is to teach that subject (e.g., English majors become English teachers; history majors become history teachers). However, the truth is that students majoring in liberal arts fields enter, advance, and prosper in a wide variety of careers. Among students with liberal arts majors are such notable college graduates as:

- Jill Barad (English major), CEO, Mattel Toys
- Steve Case (political science major), CEO, America Online
- Brian Lamb (speech major), CEO, C-Span
- Willie Brown (liberal studies major), Mayor, San Francisco (74).

Significant numbers of liberal arts majors are employed in positions that involve marketing, human resources, or public affairs (23, 157). Research also reveals that the career mobility and career advancement of liberal arts majors working in the corporate world are comparable to business majors. For example, liberal arts majors are just as likely to advance to the highest levels of corporate leadership as majors in pre-professional fields such as business and engineering (127).

Students majoring in a liberal arts field can further increase their marketability by combining their major with a minor or cluster of courses in a more "applied" pre-professional field. For example, students majoring in the fine arts (music, theatre) or humanities (English, history) may take courses in the fields of mathematics (e.g., statistics), technology (e.g., computer science), and business (e.g., economics) to acquire knowledge and skills that are not typically emphasized by their major. (Some campuses offer business courses that are reserved specifically for liberal arts majors.) Employment and career opportunities for non-business majors are enhanced if they have some course work in business (e.g., economics, business administration) (149). Liberal arts majors can further increase their employment prospects by completing an internship. Research shows that students in all majors who have an internship while in college are more likely to develop career-relevant work skills and find immediate employment after graduation (127).

Furthermore, liberal arts majors are not restricted to pursuing a degree in graduate school or professional school that is in the same field as their college major. For example, English majors can still go to graduate school in an academic field other than English, or go to law school, or get a master's degree in business administration. In fact, it is common to find that the majority of graduate students in master's of business administration (MBA) programs were not business majors (51).

The liberal arts broaden, rather than narrow, your future career possibilities. If you have a passion for and talent in a liberal arts field, do not be dismayed or discouraged by those who may question your choice by asking: "What are you going to do with a degree in *that* major?"

Journal Entry 1.1

How would you interpret the meaning or message of the following quotes?

"It is such good fortune for people in power that people do not think."

—Adolf Hitler, German dictator

"Those who cannot remember the past are damned to repeat it."

—George Santayana, Spanish-born American philosopher

"A liberal [arts] education frees a person from the prison-house of class, race, time, place, background, family, and nation."

—Robert Hutchins, former dean of Yale Law School and president of the University of Chicago

Journal Entry 1.2

I am going to college to …

I decided to attend this particular college or university because . . .

Journal Entry 1.3

What would you say in response to a classmate who asks you the following question: "Aren't you glad to get all your general education (liberal arts) courses out of the way and over with, so you can finally get into courses that actually relate to your major and future career?"

Journal Entry 1.4

Reflect on your responses to the reflection questions in this chapter. Which one(s) do you find to be most personally significant or revealing? Why?

Exercise 1.1 Developing a General Education Plan for Making the Most of the Liberal Arts

Highlight the specific courses in the catalog that you plan to take to fulfill your general education requirements in each area of the liberal arts. Before making a course selection, carefully read the description of the course in your college catalog or bulletin.

Select general education courses that will enable you to attain all of the *broadening perspectives* developed by a liberal arts education. For example, strategically select courses that provide you with a *societal* perspective (e.g., sociology), a *national* perspective (e.g., political science), an *international* perspective (e.g., cultural geography), and a *global* perspective (e.g., ecology). (All of the broadening perspectives developed by the liberal arts are described on pages 13.)

Exercise

Use the form below as a checklist to ensure that all key perspectives are included and that there are no "blind spots" in your general education plan.

Broadening Social-Spatial Perspectives (See pp. 9–13 for further descriptions of these perspectives.)	Course Developing This Perspective (Read the course descriptions in your Catalog to identify a general education requirement that develops each of these perspectives.)
Self	
Family	
Community	
Society	
Culture	
Nation	
International	
Global	
Universe (Cosmos)	
Broadening Chronological Perspectives (See pp. 14–17 for detailed description of these perspectives.)	**Course Developing This Perspective** (Read the course descriptions in your Catalog to identify a general education requirement that develops each of these perspectives.)
Historical	
Contemporary	
Futuristic	

Select general education courses that will enable you to develop yourself as a *whole person*. Enroll in courses that cover all the key dimensions of self-development and allow you to develop as a whole person. For instance, include courses that promote your *emotional* development (e.g., stress management), *social* development (e.g., interpersonal relationships), *mental* development (e.g., critical thinking), *physical* development (e.g., nutrition, self-defense), and *spiritual* development (e.g., world religions; death and dying).

Remember that development of the "whole self" also includes co-curricular learning experiences outside the classroom (e.g., leadership and volunteer experiences). Be sure to include these experiences as part of your holistic-development plan. Your student handbook probably represents the best resource for information about co-curricular experiences offered by your college.

Use the form below as a checklist below for ensuring that your educational plan includes all key elements of holistic ("whole person") development.

Dimensions of Self (See pp. 16–17 for description of these dimensions.)	Course or Co-curricular Experience Developing this Dimension of Self (Consult your student handbook for co-curricular experiences.)
Intellectual (Cognitive)	
Emotional	
Social	
Ethical	
Physical	
Spiritual	
Vocational	
Personal	

CHAPTER 2

Diversity and Its Relationship to the Liberal Arts

Reflection 2.1

Please complete the following sentence:
When I hear the word "diversity," the first thoughts that come to my mind are …

The word *diversity* derives from the Latin root "diversus," meaning variation or various. Thus, human diversity refers to the variation that exists among people that comprise humanity (the human species). As depicted in **Figure 2.1**, the relationship between humanity and diversity is similar to the relationship between sunlight and the spectrum of colors. Similar to sunlight passing through a prism is dispersed into all the different groups of colors that comprise the visual spectrum, the human

> "We are all brothers and sisters. Each face in the rainbow of color that populates our world is precious and special. Each adds to the rich treasure of humanity."
> —Morris Dees, civil rights leader and co-founder of the Southern Poverty Law Center

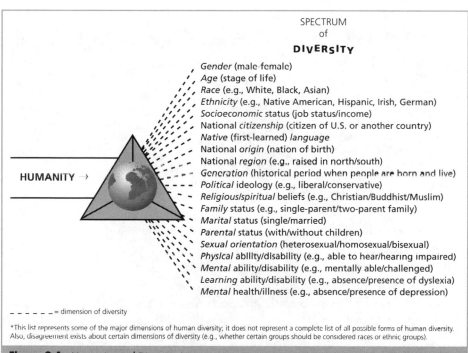

SPECTRUM
of
DIVERSITY

HUMANITY →

Gender (male-female)
Age (stage of life)
Race (e.g., White, Black, Asian)
Ethnicity (e.g., Native American, Hispanic, Irish, German)
Socioeconomic status (job status/income)
National *citizenship* (citizen of U.S. or another country)
Native (first-learned) *language*
National *origin* (nation of birth)
National *region* (e.g., raised in north/south)
Generation (historical period when people are born and live)
Political ideology (e.g., liberal/conservative)
Religious/spiritual beliefs (e.g., Christian/Buddhist/Muslim)
Family status (e.g., single-parent/two-parent family)
Marital status (single/married)
Parental status (with/without children)
Sexual orientation (heterosexual/homosexual/bisexual)
Physical ability/disability (e.g., able to hear/hearing impaired)
Mental ability/disability (e.g., mentally able/challenged)
Learning ability/disability (e.g., absence/presence of dyslexia)
Mental health/illness (e.g., absence/presence of depression)

– – – – – – = dimension of diversity

*This list represents some of the major dimensions of human diversity; it does not represent a complete list of all possible forms of human diversity. Also, disagreement exists about certain dimensions of diversity (e.g., whether certain groups should be considered as races or ethnic groups).

Figure 2.1. Humanity and Diversity.*

species spread across planet earth is dispersed into all the different groups of people that comprise the human spectrum (humanity).

As you can see in **Figure 2.1**, humans differ from one another in a wide variety of ways, including physical features, religious beliefs, mental and physical abilities, national origins, social backgrounds, gender, sexual orientation, and a variety of other personal dimensions.

Reflection 2.2

Look over the list of groups that comprise the diversity spectrum in **Figure 2.1**. Do you notice any groups that are missing from the list that should be added, either because they have distinctive backgrounds or because they have been targets of prejudice and discrimination?

> Diversity is a human issue that embraces and benefits all people; it is not a code word that stands for "some people."

> "Diversity is a value that is shown in mutual respect and appreciation of similarities and differences."
> –Public Service Enterprise Group

It is important to remember that human *variety* and human *similarity* exist side by side together and complement one another. Studying diversity not only enhances our appreciation of the unique features of different cultures; it also gives us insight into the universal aspects of the human experience that are common to all human beings—regardless of their particular social or cultural background. For example, despite our racial and ethnic differences, all humans experience the same emotions and express them with the same facial expressions (see **Figure 2.2**).

Reflection 2.3

List three human experiences that are universal—i.e., that all humans experience in all cultures.

    1.

    2.

    3.

> Diversity represents variations on the common theme of humanity. Although we have different cultural backgrounds, those differences are still cultivated from the same soil — they are all grounded in the common experience of being human.

Other human characteristics that anthropologists have found to be shared across all groups of people in every corner of the world include storytelling, poetry, adornment of the body, dance, music, decoration of artifacts, families, socialization of children by elders, a sense of right and wrong, supernatural beliefs, explanations of diseases and death, and mourning of the dead (131). Although different ethnic groups may express these shared human experiences in different ways, these are universal experiences common to all human beings.

Human languages provide an excellent example of the relationship between humanity and diversity. Although humans across the world speak different languages, all newborn babies in all cultures babble with the same sounds and they are sounds used in all human languages. However, what particular babbling sounds they will continue to use depends on the language they are exposed to in their culture.

Humans all over the world display the same facial expressions when experiencing certain emotions.
See if you can detect the emotions being expressed in the following faces.
(To find the answers, turn your book upside down.)

Answers: The emotions shown. Top, left to right: anger, fear, and sadness.
Bottom, left to right: disgust, happiness, and surprise.

All images © JupiterImages Corporation.

Figure 2.2. Human Facial Expressions.

Human infants will hold on to the babbling sounds that they hear spoken in their particular culture; the other babbling sounds will drop out of their oral repertoire (123). The fact that all humans express themselves with the same set of sounds at birth (our "universal language") reflects our common humanity; the different set of sounds that humans eventually learn to use when speaking their "native language" reflect our cultural diversity.

Thus, the cultures associated with different ethnic groups may be viewed simply as variations on the same theme: being human. You may have heard people say: "We're all human, aren't we?" The answer to this important question is, "Yes and no."

To appreciate diversity and its relationship with humanity is to capitalize on the power of our differences (diversity) while still preserving our collective strength through unity (humanity).

We are all the same, but not in the same way. A good metaphor for understanding this apparent contradiction is to visualize humanity as a quilt in which we are all joined together by the common thread of humanity—by the common bond of being human. The different patches that comprise the quilt represent diversity—the distinctive cultures that comprise our common humanity. The quilt metaphor acknowledges the identity and beauty of all cultures and differs radically from the old American "melting pot" metaphor, which viewed differences as something that should be melted down or eliminated; it also differs from the later "salad bowl" metaphor, which suggested that America is a hodgepodge or mishmash of different cultures thrown together without any common connection. In contrast, the quilt metaphor implies that the different cultural groups should be recognized and celebrated. At the same time, these cultural differences can be woven together to create a single, unified whole. This view of the relationship between diversity and unity is reflected by the Latin expression: *E pluribus Unum* (out of many, one)—the motto of the United States that appears on all its coins.

PERSONAL EXPERIENCE | Joe Cuseo

When I was twelve years old and living in New York City, I returned from school one Friday afternoon and my mother asked me if anything interesting happened at school that day. I mentioned to her that the teacher went around the room, asking students what we had for dinner the night before. At that moment, my mother began to become a bit concerned and nervously asked me: "What did you tell the teacher?" I said: "I told her and the rest of the class that I had pasta last night because my family always eats pasta on Thursdays and Sundays." My mother exploded and fired back at me: "Why couldn't you tell her that we had steak or roast beef!" For a moment, I was stunned and couldn't figure out what I had done wrong or why I should have lied about eating pasta. Then it suddenly dawned on me: My mother was embarrassed about being an Italian American. She wanted me to hide our family's ethnic background and make it sound like we were very "American." After this became clear to me, a few moments later, it also became clear to me why her maiden name was changed from the very Italian-sounding "DeVigilio" to the more American-sounding "Vigilis," why her first name was changed from Carmella to Mildred, and why my father's first name was also changed from Biaggio to Blase. Their generation wanted to minimize the risk of being seen as different and being discriminated against, while maximizing their assimilation (absorption) into American culture.

I never forgot this incident because it was such an eye-opening experience for a young boy. For the first time in my life, I became aware that my mother was ashamed of being a member of the same group to which every other member of my family belonged, including me. After her outburst, I felt a combined rush of astonishment and embarrassment. These feelings eventually faded and my mother's reaction ended up having the opposite effect on me. Instead of making me feel inferior or ashamed about being Italian-American, her reaction that day caused me to become more conscious of, and take more pride in, my Italian heritage.

As I grew older, I also grew to understand why my mother felt the way she did. She grew up in the era of the America's "melting pot"—a time when different American ethnic groups were expected to melt down and melt away their ethnicity. They were not to celebrate diversity; they were to eliminate it.

What Is Racial Diversity?

Humanity embraces both ethnic and racial diversity. Whereas members of an ethnic group share a common culture that has been learned through shared social experiences, members of a *racial* group share common *physical* characteristics (e.g., skin color or facial features) that have been inherited biologically. The U.S. Census Bureau 2000 (154) identifies three races: White, Black, and Asian. However, as Anderson and Fienberg, 2000 (7) caution us, racial categories are social-political constructs (mentally created categories), not scientific concepts. Scholars still disagree about what groups of people actually constitute a human "race," or whether totally distinctive races truly exist (161). There are no specific genes that differentiate one race from another; in other words, there is no way you could do a blood test or any type of "internal" genetic test to determine a person's race.

Although humans display diversity in skin color or tone, the reality is that all members of the human species are remarkably similar biologically. Over 98 percent of the genes that make up humans from different racial groups are exactly the same (27, 105). This extraordinarily large amount of genetic overlap among all human beings accounts for the many similarities that exist among us, despite these differences in color that appear at the surface of our skin. For example, all humans have similar external features that give us a "human" appearance and clearly distinguish us from other animal species. All humans have internal organs that are similar in structure and function; and no matter what the color of our outer layer of skin, when it's cut, we all bleed in the same color.

Humans have simply decided to categorize themselves into "races" on the basis of certain external differences in their appearance, particularly the color of their outer layer of skin. The U.S. Census Bureau could just as easily have divided us into categories based on other physical characteristics, such as eye color (blue, brown, green) or hair texture (straight, wavy, curly, frizzy).

> "We have become not a melting pot but a beautiful mosaic."
>
> Jimmy Carter, thirty-ninth president of the United States and winner of the Nobel Peace Prize

My father stood approximately six feet and had light brown straight hair. His skin color was that of a Western European with a very slight suntan. My mother was from Alabama and she was dark in skin color with high cheek bones and long curly black hair. In fact, if you did not know that my father was of African-American descent, you would not have thought of him as black. All of my life I have thought of myself as African American and all of the people who are familiar with me thought of me as African American. I have lived half of a century with that as my racial identity. Several years ago, after carefully looking through available records on births in my family history, I discovered that less than 50 percent of my lineage was African. Biologically, I am not black. Socially and emotionally, I am. Clearly, race is more of a socially constructed concept than a biologically based fact.

The differences in skin color among humans we see today are likely due to biological adaptations that evolved over thousands of years among human groups who lived in very different regions of the world. Darker skin tones likely developed among humans who inhabited and reproduced in hotter regions nearer the equator (e.g., African), where their darker skin evolved to help them adapt and survive by providing their bodies with better protection from the potentially damaging effects of the sun (27) and by allowing their bodies to make efficient use of vitamin D supplied by sunlight (75). In contrast, lighter skin tones developed over time among humans inhabiting colder climates farther from the equator (e.g., Scandinavia) so their bodies could absorb greater amounts of sunlight—which was in shorter supply in that region of the world.

I was proofreading this chapter while sitting in a coffee shop in Chicago O'Hare Airport. I looked up from my work for a second and saw that appeared to be a white girl about eighteen years old. As I lowered by head to return to my work, I did a double-take to look at her again because something about her seemed different or unusual. When I looked at her more closely the second time, I noticed that although she had white skin, the features of her face and hair appeared to be those of an African-American. After a couple of seconds of puzzlement, I figured it out: she was an *albino* African-American. That satisfied me for the moment, and I returned to my work; however, I later began to wonder whether it would still be accurate to say that she was "black" because her skin was actually white. Would her hair and facial features be sufficient for her to be considered (or classified) as black? If yes, then what about someone who had black skin tone, but did not have the typical hair and facial features that are characteristic of black people? Is skin color the defining factor or feature of being African-American, or are other features equally important? I was unable to answer these questions, but I found it amusing that all of these thoughts were taking place while I was working on a book dealing with diversity. Later, on the plane ride home, I thought again about that albino African-American girl and realized that she was a perfect example of how classifying people into "races" is not based on objective, scientifically determined evidence, but on subjective, socially-constructed categories.

Reflection 2.4

What race do you consider yourself to be? Would you say you identify strongly with your race, or are you rarely conscious of it? Why?

Diversity Further Broadens the Perspectives Developed by the Liberal Arts

As discussed in Chapter 1, the liberal arts broaden your perspective to include other people, places, and times. Diversity further extends the broadening perspectives of the liberal arts further by exposing you to the variety of sub-perspectives found within each broadening perspective of the liberal arts.

What follows is a discussion of the diverse perspectives embedded within each of the perspectives of people, places, and times developed by the liberal arts. It could be said the each broadening perspective of the liberal arts is a general theme and the diversity of sub-perspectives threaded within each of them are specific variations on that general theme.

Diversity and the Perspective of the Individual (Self)

It is important to keep in mind the differences among individuals *within* a particular ethnic and racial groups are *greater* than the average differences between different groups. For example, although we live in a world that is very conscious of racial differences based on skin color, the truth is that individuals of the same race differ more in their physical characteristics (e.g., height and weight) and personality characteristics (e.g., introverts and extroverts) than the average difference between races in height, weight, or personality (34). In other words, individual differences are greater than group differences.

Thus, humankind can be viewed and understood from three different perspectives:

1. **Humanity:** All humans are members of the *same group* (the human species).
2. **Diversity:** All humans are members of *different groups* (e.g., different gender and ethnic groups).

> "Every human is, at the same time, like all other humans, like some humans, and like no other human."
>
> —Clyde Kluckholn, American anthropologist

3. **Individuality:** Each human is a *unique individual* who is different than all other humans and all other members of any group to which that individual may belong.

Diversity and the Perspective of Family

To fully understand the family perspective developed by the liberal arts is to appreciate diversity of human families. Family forms in a wide variety of ways—as illustrated by the following lengthy list.

- **Nuclear families:** Consist of two spouses and one or more children.
- **Extended families:** Include members who are biologically related to the nuclear family (e.g., grandparents, uncles, aunts, adult children).
- **Families with children.**
- **Families without children.**
- **Single-parent families:** Consist of one parent and at least one child.
- **Patriarchal families:** The family's major authority figure or decision-maker is the father.
- **Matriarchal families:** The family's major authority figure or decision-maker is the mother.
- **Single-income families:** Contain only one "breadwinner" (wage earner).
- **Multi-ethnic families:** Include members from more than one ethnic group.
- **Multi-racial families:** Include members from more than one racial group.
- **Blended families:** Contain two or more siblings who are unrelated biologically, but who become members of the same family through remarriage one of their biological parents.
- **Step families:** Contain children living with one biological parent and that parent's current spouse or partner who is biologically unrelated to the child.
- **Families with adopted children.**
- **Families comprised of unmarried partners.**
- **Families comprised of gay partners.**

As the above list demonstrates, gaining a comprehensive perspective on the family requires taking multiple sub-perspectives that involve diverse social arrangements.

Reflection 2.5

Which of the above family arrangements most closely corresponds to the one in which you were raised? In what way(s) do you think your family structure affected your development and the person you are today? Why?

The following charts provide a statistical summary of family diversity in America.

Household Types 1990–2000

	1990 Number	Percent	2000 Number	Percent
Total Households	**91,947,410**	**100.00%**	**105,480,101**	**100.00%**
Married Couple	**50,708,322**	**55.15%**	**54,493,232**	**51.66%**
With Children*	23,494,726	25.55%	24,835,505	23.55%
Without Children*	27,213,596	29.60%	29,657,727	28.12%
Female Householder, No Spouse	**10,666,043**	**11.60%**	**12,900,103**	**12.23%**
With Children*	6,028,409	6.56%	7,561,874	7.17%
Without Children*	4,637,634	5.04%	5,338,229	5.06%
Male Householder, No Spouse	**3,143,582**	**3.42%**	**4,394,012**	**4.17%**
With Children*	1,354,540	1.47%	2,190,989	2.08%
Without Children*	1,789,042	1.95%	2,203,023	2.09%
Non-Family Households	**27,429,463**	**29.83%**	**33,692,754**	**31.94%**
Living Alone	22,580,420	24.56%	27,230,075	25.82%
Two o More Persons	4,849,043	5.27%	6,462,679	6.13%

*In this table, children are people under age 18.
Source: "Census 2000" analyzed by the Social Science Data Analysis Network (SSDAN).

Multiracial Households (In rank order of the top 20)

Rank	Multiple Race Selection	Percent of Total Number	Percent of Multiple Race Population	Population
1.	White and Some Other Race	2,206,251	0.78%	32.32%
2.	White and American Indian	1,082,683	0.38%	15.86%
3.	White and Asian	868,395	0.31%	12.72%
4.	White and Black	784,764	0.28%	11.50%
5.	Black and Some Other Race	417,249	0.15%	6.11%
6.	Asian and Some other Race	249,108	0.09%	3.65%
7.	Black and American Indian	182,494	0.06%	2.67%
8.	Asian and Hawaiian or Other Pacific Islander	138,802	0.05%	2.03%
9.	White and Hawaiian or Other Pacific Islander	112,964	0.04%	1.65%
10.	White and Black and American Indian	112,207	0.04%	1.64%
11.	Black and Asian	106,782	0.04%	1.56%
12.	American Indian and Some Other Race	93,842	0.03%	1.37%
13.	White and Asian and Hawaiian or Other Pacific Islander	89,611	0.03%	1.31%
14.	American Indian and Asian	52,429	0.02%	0.77%
15.	White and Black and Some Other Race	43,172	0.02%	0.63%

(continued)

Multiracial Households (In rank order of the top 20) (continued)				
Rank	Multiple Race Selection	Percent of total Number	Percent of Multiple Race Population	Population
16.	Hawaiian or Other Pacific Islander and Some Other Race	35,108	0.01%	0.51%
17.	White and Asian and Some Other Race	34,962	0.01%	0.51%
18.	Black and Hawaiian or Other pacific Islander	29,876	0.01%	0.44%
19.	White and American Indian and Some Other Race	29,095	0.01%	0.43%
20.	White and American Indian and Asian	23,766	0.01%	0.35%

Source: "Census 2000" analyzed by the Social Science Data Analysis Network (SSDAN).

Diversity and the Perspective of Community

People of character are good *citizens*. They model what it means to live in a community by displaying *civility*—they are respectful of and sensitive to the rights of others. In exercising their own rights and freedoms, they do not step on (or stomp on) the rights and freedoms of others. Civically responsible people treat fellow community members in a humane and compassionate manner, and are willing to challenge those who violate the rights of others. Humans with civic character are model citizens whose actions visibly demonstrate to others that they actively oppose any attempts to disrespect or dehumanize fellow members of their community.

Diversity and the Societal Perspective

American society is more ethnically and racially diverse than at any other time in history and it will continue to grow more diverse throughout the twenty-first century (151). For example, in 1995, 75 percent of America's population was white; by 2050, it will shrink to 50 percent (155). These demographic changes are creating an increasingly multicultural society in which the ability to understand, relate to, and learn from others of diverse racial and ethnic backgrounds is an essential skill for both personal and professional success (145, 11).

Significant diversity also exists in income level among different groups of people in American society. For example, sharp differences in income level exist between different racial and ethnic groups. In 2007, black households had the lowest median income ($33,916)—compared to a median income of $54,920 for non-Hispanic white households (156). Poverty remains a persistent problem in the United States. In 2007, 12.5 percent or 37.3 million Americans lived in poverty, making the United States one of the most impoverished of all developed countries in the world (142). People of color have higher rates of poverty (154), and people who live in poverty are more likely to be targets of discrimination (96). Poverty also strikes American unequally in different regions: South (14.2%), West (12%), Northeast (11.4%), and Midwest (11.1%) (156).

Thus, to gain a comprehensive understanding of the societal perspective developed by the liberal arts requires appreciation of differences in race, ethnicity, and socioeconomic status.

Diversity and the Perspective of Culture

As discussed in Chapter 1, culture may be broadly defined as a distinctive pattern of beliefs and values that are learned by a group of people who share the same social heritage and traditions. Diversity across ethnic (cultural) groups is expressed in a wide variety of ways, which include variations with respect to the following key components of culture:

- **Language:** How a culture communicates verbally and nonverbally (e.g., the extent and nature of body language used while communicating).

- **Space (Distance):** How a cultural group prefers to arrange its members with respect to space or physical distance (e.g., how closely they position themselves to one another other when they engage in conversation).

- **Time:** How a cultural group conceives of, divides, and uses time (e.g., the speed or pace at which they conduct business).

- **Aesthetics:** How a culture appreciates and expresses artistic beauty and creativity (e.g., visual art, culinary art, music, theater, literature, and dance).

- **Family:** Cultural attitudes and habits with respect to raising children and treating the elderly (e.g., customary style of parenting children and caring for aging parents).

- **Finances:** How a cultural group meets its members' material wants and its habits with respect to acquiring wealth and spending money (e.g., its emphasis on material possessions and the extent to which those possessions should be flaunted).

- **Science and Technology:** Cultural attitude toward and use of science or technology in its day-to-day activities (e.g. whether or not the culture is technologically "advanced").

- **Philosophy:** Cultural views on what constitutes wisdom, truth, goodness, and the meaning or purpose of life (e.g., its predominant ethical viewpoints and values).

- **Religion:** Cultural beliefs about a supreme being and the afterlife (e.g., heaven, hell, or reincarnation).

Reflection 2.6

Look back the key components mentioned in the above list. Think of another component of culture that you think is important or influential and add it to the list. Explain why you think this is an important element of a group's culture.

All of these cultural differences can exist within the same society (a multicultural society), within the same nation (domestic diversity), and across different nations (international diversity). The major cultural (ethnic) groups found within the United States include:

- Native Americans (American Indians)
  o Cherokee, Navaho, Hopi, Alaskan natives, Blackfoot, etc.
- African Americans (Blacks)
  o Americans whose cultural roots lie in the continent of Africa, the Caribbean Islands, etc.
- Hispanic Americans (Latinos)
  o Americans with cultural roots in Mexico, Puerto Rico, Central America, South America, etc.
- Asian Americans
  o Americans with cultural roots in Japan, China, Korea, Vietnam, etc.
- European Americans (Whites)
  o Descendents from different regions of Europe (England, Ireland, Germany, Scandinavia, Italy, etc.)

Currently, European Americans represent the *majority* ethnic group in the United States, accounting for more than one-half of the American population. Native Americans, African Americans, Hispanic Americans, and Asian Americans are considered to be ethnic *minority* groups because each of these groups represents less than 50 percent of the American population.

As with the concept of race, classifying a particular group of people as an ethnic group can be very arbitrary, subjective, and interpreted differently by different groups of people. Currently, the only races recognized by the U.S. Census Bureau are white, black, and Asian. Hispanic is not currently defined as a race, but is classified as an ethnic group; however, among those who checked "some other race" in the 2000 Census, 97 percent were Hispanic. This finding suggests that Hispanic Americans consider themselves to be a racial group rather than an ethnic (cultural) group, perhaps because this is how they see non-Hispanics perceive and treat them (36).

This illustrates how difficult it is to categorize people into particular racial or ethnic groups. The United States will continue to struggle with the classification issue because the ethnic and racial diversity of its population is growing, and members of different ethnic and racial groups are forming cross-ethnic and inter-racial families. For example, by 2050, the number of Americans who will identify themselves as being of two or more races is projected to more than triple, growing from 5.2 million to 16.2 million (156). Thus, it will become progressively more difficult to place Americans into distinct categories based on their race or ethnicity.

As the child of a black man and a white woman, and as someone born in the racial melting pot of Hawaii, with a sister who's half Indonesian but who's usually mistaken for Mexican or Puerto Rican, and a brother-in-law and niece of Chinese descent, with some blood relatives who resemble Margaret Thatcher and others who could pass for Bernie Mac, family get-togethers over Christmas take on the appearance of a UN General Assembly meeting. I've never had the option of restricting my loyalties on the basis of race, or measuring my worth on the basis of tribe.

Reflection 2.7

What ethnic group(s) are you a member of, or do you identify with? What cultural values do you think are shared by your ethnic group(s)?

Diversity and the National Perspective

America is rapidly becoming a more racially and ethnically diverse nation. In 2008, the minority population in the U.S. reached an all-time high of 34 percent of the total population. The population of ethnic minorities is now growing at a much faster rate than the white majority, and this trend is expected to continue. By the middle of the twenty-first century, the minority population will have grown from one-third of the U.S. population to more than one-half (54 percent), with more than and 60 percent of the nation's children expected to be members of minority groups (156).

The rise in ethnic and racial diversity in America as a nation is reflected on its college campuses. This diversity is particularly noteworthy when viewed in light of the historical treatment of minority groups in the United States. In the early nineteenth century, education was not a right, but a privilege available only to those who could afford to attend private schools. Members of certain minority groups were left out of the educational process altogether, or were forced to be educated in racially segregated settings. Americans of color were once taught in separate, segregated schools that were typically inferior in terms of educational facilities. The groundbreaking Supreme Court ruling in *Brown vs. Board of Education* (1954) changed the face of education for people of color by ruling that "separate educational facilities are inherently unequal." The decision made it illegal for Kansas and twenty other states to deliver education in segregated classrooms.

For the first time in America's history, the diversity of students on American college campuses is now making real the original ideal of the liberal arts—to provide a liberating education for *all* Americans—regardless of their culture, color, creed, or gender (11).

"Of all the civil rights for which the world has struggled and fought for 5,000 years, the right to learn is undoubtedly the most fundamental."
–W. E. B. Du Bois, African-American sociologist, historian, and civil rights activist

"Americanism is a question of principles, of idealism, of character: it is not a matter of birthplace or creed or line of descent."
–Theodore Roosevelt, American soldier, president, and Nobel Prize winner

In 2009, an African American was elected President of the United States for the first time in the nation's history. As a person who grew up in an environment and during times where history books only discussed African Americans in terms of slave roles, this is very much a historic occasion. As an African American who is the great grandson of slaves, this is a time that I did not think I would see in my lifetime. However, the success of this candidate reached across many diverse lines: generational, racial, ethnic, religious, socioeconomic, political party affiliation, etc. Although we have a long way to go to break down all the barriers that keep us separated in this country, I am an American who is very proud today to see a new chapter added to the American Dream. In fact, all of America should be proud that we expressed our diversity in action and moved America one step forward in our global family.

Diversity and the International Perspective

International interdependence among nations is growing as a result of advances in communication technology, international travel, and multinational corporations. As a result, international knowledge and cross-cultural competences have become essential for career advancement in today's world and for addressing its most serious problems (e.g., international terrorism). America, in particular, is a nation whose interests, attitudes and values strongly influence those of other nations. The scope of this influence is captured by the following personal experience.

How much are we in America aware of the influence of our values and way of behaving on others? I have learned that the most popular TV show among pre-teenagers in many countries is "The Simpsons," and American movies and our culture artists have an increasing influence abroad. A growing number of young people in other countries are now "binge drinking," previously only an American phenomenon. Are we part of the problem or the solution?

American college students lag behind students from other industrialized nations in international knowledge and skills (23). Only 5–10 percent of American college graduates have basic competence in any language other than English, and approximately two-thirds of them have not taken a single course in international studies (2). Thus, the need for college graduates to acquire an international perspective and diversity-related skills that develop cross-cultural awareness is probably more important today than at any other time in the history of American higher education.

Diversity and the Global Perspective

To take a global perspective is to appreciate the diversity of humankind. If it were possible to reduce the world's population to a "village" of precisely 100 people while keeping its proportions of human diversity exactly the same, the demographics of this global village would look something like this:

60 Asians, 14 Africans, 12 Europeans, 8 Latin Americans, 5 from the United States and Canada, and 1 from the South Pacific

51 males and 49 females

82 non-whites and 18 whites

67 non-Christians and 33 Christians

80 living in substandard housing

67 unable to read

50 malnourished and 1 dying of starvation

33 without access to a safe water supply

39 without access to sufficient sanitation

24 without any electricity, and among the 76 with electricity, most would only be able to use it for light at night

7 with access to the Internet

1 with a college education

1 with HIV

2 near birth and 1 near death

5 control 32 percent of the entire world's wealth; all 5 are citizens of the United States

33 attempt to live on just 3 percent of the village's total income

(*Source: State of the Village Report* by Donella H. Meadows updated in Family Care Foundation, 2005. (56))

Furthermore, as can be seen in **Figure 2.3**, English would not be the most common language spoken in this global village.

Reflection 2.8

Look back at the characteristics of the global village on page 45. Which characteristic(s) of it surprised you? Why?

A global perspective also goes beyond human diversity to embrace appreciation of *biodiversity*—variations in all life forms inhabiting planet Earth. Biodiversity can only take place if there is *ecosystem* diversity, i.e., when all the biological, climatic, geological, and chemical ingredients in the environment combine to maintain the life of plants and animals, whose life needs are met by interacting with all parts of the environmental system (119). Thus, the contemporary issue of environmental

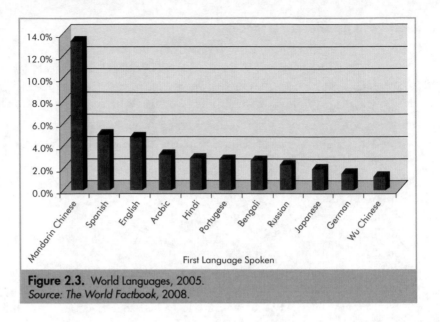

Figure 2.3. World Languages, 2005.
Source: The World Factbook, 2008.

sustainability is actually a diversity issue that embraces both ecosystem diversity and, ultimately, biodiversity. The worldwide significance of this issue is highlighted by the fact that 2010 was declared by the United Nations as the "International Year of Biodiversity" (IYB) to raise global awareness that preservation of biodiversity requires the collective effort of every nation and all humankind (152).

Diversity and the Universe (Cosmos)

Human diversity on planet earth is accompanied by cosmic diversity in the universe. Lest we forget, Earth is only one planet (the "third stone from the sun") sharing a solar system with seven other planets, and it is only one celestial body sharing a galaxy with millions of other celestial bodies, including stars, moons, meteorites, and asteroids (55).

Diversity and the Chronological (Temporal) Perspective

As discussed in Chapter 1, the liberal arts not only expand your perspective to embrace different people and different places, they also expand your perspective of time by providing you with a **chronological perspective** that embraces the past, present, and future. Diversity enriches the chronological perspective by enabling you to gain a cross-cultural perspective on the concept of time. For example, Western cultures—such as the United States and Canada—take a "monochronic" perspective on time that focuses heavily on the present (the "here and now") and deals with events one at a time. In contrast, Eastern cultures—such as India and China—take a "polychromic" perspective that doesn't divide time into discrete, separate segments (past, present, future). Instead, Eastern cultures tend to view time in terms of a spectrum or continuum, along which past, present, and future merge together to form a continuous flow of interdependent events (91, 120).

In addition to expanding our perspective on time, diversity also deepens our understanding of each of the three major chronological perspectives developed by the liberal arts: historical, contemporary, and futuristic.

Diversity and the Historical Perspective

Incorporating diversity into our historical perspective serves to elevate our awareness of the struggles that different groups of people have endured to gain personal freedom, human rights, and social justice. For instance, a historical perspective leads to a clearer understanding of current-day concepts of race and racism. The expression "white race" did not exist until it was introduced by Americans in the eighteenth and nineteenth centuries. Up to that point in time, the term was not used anywhere else in the world. The success of the American cotton industry increased the need for Native American land and African American slaves. To meet their needs for land and labor, the white Anglo-Protestant upper class created and disseminated the idea of a privileged white race that was entitled to enslave people of color. Thus, the concept of a white race was originally devised by English settlers to gain socioeconomic advantages and to justify enslavement of African and Native Americans—who were deemed to be "uncivilized savages." Subsequent waves of American immigrants who initially defined themselves as German, Irish, or Italian gradually began to refer to themselves as white as they began to move up to higher levels of socioeconomic and political status (57).

"The Constitution of the United States knows no distinction between citizens on account of color."

–Frederick Douglass, abolitionist, author, advocate for equal rights for all people, and former slave

---

PERSONAL EXPERIENCE | Aaron Thompson

My mother was a direct descendent of slaves and moved with her parents from the deep south at the age of seventeen. My father lived in an all-black coal mining camp, into which my mother and her family moved in 1938. My father remained illiterate because he was not allowed to attend public schools in eastern Kentucky.

In the early 1960s my brother, my sister, and I were integrated into the white public schools. Physical violence and constant verbal harassment caused many other blacks to forgo their education and opt for jobs in the coal mines at an early age. But my father remained constant in his advice to me: "It doesn't matter if they call you n____; but don't you ever let them beat you by walking out on your education."

My dad would say to me, "Son, you will have opportunities that I never had. Many people, white and black alike, will tell you that you are no good and that education can never help you. Don't listen to them because soon they will not be able to keep you from getting an education like they did me. Just remember,

(continued)

when you do get that education, you'll never have to go in those coal mines and have them break your back. You can choose what you want to do, and then you can be a free man."

Being poor, black, and Appalachian did not offer me great odds for success, but constant reminders from my parents that I was a good and valuable person helped me to look beyond my deterrents and see the true importance of education. My parents, who could never provide me with monetary wealth, provided me with the gift of motivation and aspiration for achievement.

As this personal story illustrates, humans are also diverse with respect to the historical time period during which they grew up. The term "generation" refers to a group of human beings that is born during the same historical period and who develop similar attitudes, values and habits because they experienced similar world events during their formative years of development. **Box 2.1** provides a brief summary of the major generations that have been identified, the key historical events that occurred during their formative years of life, and the personal characteristics that have been associated or attributed to their particular generation (89).

BOX 2.1   Generational Diversity

- **The "Traditional Generation,"** *a.k.a., the "Silent Generation"* (born during the years 1922–1945). This generation was influenced by events such as the Great Depression and World Wars I and II. Characteristics associated with this generation include loyalty, patriotism, respect for authority, and conservatism.

- **The "Baby Boomer"** *Generation* (born during the years 1946–1964). This generation was influenced by events such as the Vietnam War, Watergate, and the human rights movement. The characteristics associated with this generation include idealism, concern for equal rights, and finding personal fulfillment in life.

- **"Generation X"** (born during the years 1965–1980): This generation was influenced by Sesame Street, the creation of MTV, AIDS, and soaring divorce rates—which produced the first generation of "latch-key" children—who used their own key to let themselves into their home after school because their parents, or single parent, would be working outside the home. Characteristics associated with this generation include self-reliance, resourcefulness, and being comfortable with change.

- **"Generation Y," a.k.a. "Millennials"** (born between the years 1981–2002): This generation was influenced by the 9/11 terrorist attack on the United States, the shooting of students at Columbine, and the collapse of the Enron corporation.

Characteristics associated with this generation include being skilled in computer technology, a preference for working and playing in groups, and a willingness to provide volunteer service in their community (the "civic generation"). They are also the most ethnically diverse generation, which may explain why they are more open to diversity and see it as a positive experience.

"I don't even know what that means."

—Comment made by 38-year-old basketball coach after hearing one of his younger players say: "I'm trying to find my mojo and get my swag back."

Source: Lancaster and Stillman (2002).

Diversity and the Contemporary Perspective

When diversity is viewed from a historical perspective, it is clear that progress has been made with respect to promoting social justice and appreciating human differences. However, viewing diversity from a contemporary perspective reveals that the consequences or "ripple effects" of earlier injustices still disadvantage these people today. For example, although women have won the right to vote and have gained entry into professional positions that were historically denied to them or held exclusively by men, women (as a group) still experience inequities with respect to employment compensation. American women today still earn less than American males, even if they have attained the same level of education and work experience. For instance, in 2004, women earned only seventy-seven cents to every dollar earned by men. In 2005, the median annual earnings of women ages fifteen and older were $31,858, compared to $41,386 for their male counterparts (115). Females with graduate degrees earn only slightly more than males with a high school diploma— $41,995 for women, compared to $40,822 for men (136).

Wage gaps between males and females currently exist in many professional occupations as well. In 2005, the median weekly income earned by women in the same occupation as men was significantly lower. For example, look at the gender difference in salaries between men and women in the following fields:

- **Computers and Mathematics:** Women earn 14 percent less.
- **Sales:** Women earn 37 percent less.
- **Physicians:** Women earn 39 percent less (112).

In a study conducted of management positions in ten industries that together employ over 70 percent of women in the American workforce, the male-female wage gap actually increased between 1995 and 2000 (115).

Besides pay discrepancies, inequities currently exist with respect to male-female representation in different professional fields. Although women have made great gains in certain employment in fields once dominated by males, there has never been a female president or vice president of the United States, and women still make up only approximately 25 percent of the labor force in the fields of science, technology, and engineering (38).

In addition to gender gaps in pay, wage discrimination still takes place with respect to race. As demonstrated in **Figure 2.4**, African males earn less than white Americans, even if they have attained exactly the same level of education.

Although great historical gains have been made in the equitable treatment of ethnic and racial minority groups, residential segregation still exists between groups (100, 108). Research on college campuses reveals that college students, particularly

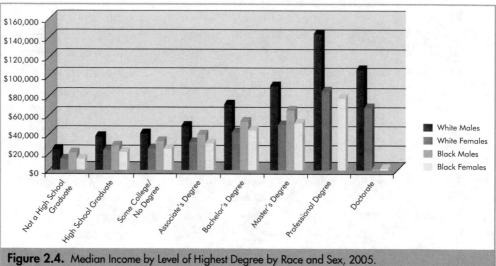

Figure 2.4. Median Income by Level of Highest Degree by Race and Sex, 2005.

white students, come from highly segregated high schools and neighborhoods (101). In a long-term study of over 2,500 first-year African-American, Asian-American, Latino, and white students at the University of Michigan, it was found that although students of color tended to segregate themselves, they were more likely to interact with white students than the reverse. White students had the most segregated friendship patterns (101).

While segregation itself may not be a blatant, malicious form of prejudice or discrimination, it can lead to reduced contact between different groups of people. This reduced contact can cause a segregated group to be viewed as "unfamiliar," and this lack of familiarity, in turn, can trigger feelings of uncertainty and anxiety toward the group (163). Since anxiety is an unpleasant emotion, when it continues to be associated with the segregated group, it can result in feelings of discomfort in the presence of members of that group and further avoidance or dislike of that group (130).

Lack of contact with other racial groups can also lead to difficulties perceiving the personal identity of individual members of the segregated group. Studies show that humans are better at recognizing members of their own race than members of other racial groups—phenomenon that scholars refer to as "own-race bias" (9). This is not caused by biological factors; it doesn't occur when members of different races have frequent contact with each other (138). Apparently, what happens when people perceive faces of individuals from unfamiliar racial groups is they fail to detect subtle differences in personal features that distinguish one individual from another; instead, these distinctive personal features are overlooked and lumped into one general race category—e.g., Asian eyes or African lips (92). Such overgeneralization has resulted in false convictions and imprisonment of innocent members of racial minority groups whom eye-witnesses from majority groups "identified" as committing a crime, but which later DNA tests proved was actually committed by a different member of the same racial group (133).

These dramatic examples of miscarriages of justice make the news. However, the less newsworthy, but more consistently negative consequence of limited contact between members of different racial (and ethnic) groups is that it increases the risk of interracial prejudice and decreases the opportunity for different racial groups to experience the benefits of diversity they have to offer one another. **Box 2.2** contains a summary of biased attitudes, prejudicial beliefs, and discriminatory behaviors that must be overcome if the full benefits of diversity are to be experienced by humankind. As you read through the list, place a checkmark next to any form of prejudice that you, a family member, or friend has experienced.

BOX 2.2   Blocks to Learning from Diversity: Biased Attitudes, Prejudicial Beliefs, and Discriminatory Behaviors

- **Stereotyping:** Viewing all individuals of the same group in the same way, i.e., as having the same qualities or characteristics.

  For example: If you're Italian, you must be in the Mafia, or have a family member who is.

- **Prejudice:** A negative pre-judgment of another group of people.

  For example: Women do not make good leaders because they are too emotional.

- **Discrimination:** Unequal and unfair treatment of a person or group of people, i.e., prejudice put into action.

  For example: People of color being paid less for performing the same job, even though they have the same level of education and job qualification as whites performing the same job.

- **Segregation:** A conscious decision of one group to separate itself (socially or physically) from another group.

  For example: "White flight"—i.e., white people departing from a neighborhood that is increasingly populated by people of color.

- **Racism:** A belief that one's race is superior to another and expression of that belief in attitude (prejudice) or action (discrimination).

  For example: Cecil Rhodes (Englishman and empire builder of British South Africa) once claimed "We [the British] are the finest race in the world and the more of the world we inhabit the better it is for the human race."

- **Institutional racism:** A subtle form of racism that is rooted in organizational policies and practices that disadvantage certain racial groups.

  For example: Race-based discrimination in mortgage lending, housing and bank loans.

- **"Jim Crow" laws:** Formal and informal laws created by whites after the abolition of slavery to segregate blacks. (The term "Jim Crow" was likely derived from a song-and-dance character named "Jump Jim Crow" who played by a white man in blackface.)

  For example: Laws requiring that blacks and whites use separate bathrooms and to be educated in separate schools.

- **Apartheid:** An institutionalized system of "legal racism" supported by a nation's government. (Apartheid derives from a word in the Afrikaan language, meaning "apartness.")

  For example: The national system of racial segregation and discrimination that existed in South Africa from 1948 to 1994.

- **Hate crimes:** Criminal action motivated solely by prejudice toward the crime victim.

  For example: Acts of vandalism or assault targeting members of a particular ethnic group or who have a particular sexual orientation.

- **Hate groups:** Organizations whose primary purpose is to stimulate prejudice, discrimination, or aggression toward certain groups of people based on their ethnicity, race, ethnicity, religion, etc.

   For example: The Ku Klux Klan—an American terrorist group that perpetrates hatred toward all non-white races.

- **Genocide:** Mass murdering of one group by another group.

   For example: The Holocaust, during World War II, when millions of Jews were systematically murdered. Other examples include the murdering of Cambodians under the Khmer Rouge regime, the murdering of Bosnian Muslims in the former country of Yugoslavia, and the slaughter of the Tutsi minority by the Hutu majority in Rwanda.

- **Classism:** Prejudice or discrimination based on social class, particularly toward people of low socioeconomic status.

   For example: Only acknowledging the contributions made by politicians and wealthy industrialists to America, while ignoring the contributions of poor immigrants, farmers, slaves, and pioneer women.

- **Religious bigotry:** Denying the fundamental human right of people to hold religious beliefs, or to hold religious beliefs that differ from one's own.

   For example: An atheist who forces non-religious (secular) beliefs on others, or a member of a religious group who believes that people who hold different religious beliefs are immoral "sinners."

- **Anti-Semitism:** Prejudice or discrimination toward Jews or people who practice the religion of Judaism.

   For example: Hating Jews because they're the ones who "killed Christ."

- **Xenophobia:** Extreme fear or hatred of foreigners, outsiders, or strangers.

   For example: Believing that all immigrants should be banned from entering the country because they will increase the crime rate.

- **Regionalism:** Prejudice or discrimination based on the geographical region in which an individual has been born and raised.

   For example: A northerner thinking that all southerners are racists.

- **Jingoism:** Excessive interest and belief in the superiority of one's own nation without acknowledging its mistakes or weaknesses (often accompanied by an aggressive foreign policy) that neglects the needs of other nations, or the common needs of all nations.

   For example: "Blind patriotism"–not seeing the shortcomings of one's own nation and viewing any questioning or criticism of their nation as disloyalty or being "unpatriotic." (As in the slogan, "America: right or wrong" or "America: love it or leave it!")

- **Terrorism:** Intentional acts of violence against civilians that are motivated by political or religious prejudice.

   For example: The September 11th attacks on the United States.

- **Sexism:** Prejudice or discrimination based on sex or gender.

  For example: Believing that no woman is fit to be president of a nation because she would be too "emotional."

- **Heterosexism:** Belief that heterosexuality is the only acceptable sexual orientation.

  For example: Using the phrase, "fag" or "queer" as an insult or put down; or believing that gays should not have the same legal rights and opportunities as heterosexuals.

- **Homophobia:** Extreme fear or hatred of homosexuals.

  For example: People who engage in "gay bashing" (acts of violence toward gays), or who create and contribute to anti-gay Web sites.

- **Ageism:** Prejudice or discrimination based on age, particularly toward the elderly.

  For example: Believing that all "old" people are bad drivers with bad memories who should not be allowed on the road.

- **Ableism:** Prejudice or discrimination toward the disabled or handicapped–physically, mentally, or emotionally.

  For example: Avoiding social contact or interaction with handicapped people.

Reflection 2.11

What form(s) of prejudice in the above list have you, a family member, or friend experienced? Why do you think it took place?

Diversity and the Futuristic Perspective

America's racial and ethnic groups, whom we now call "minorities," will be the "new majority" by the midpoint of this century (64). By 2050, the U.S. population is projected to be more than 30 percent Hispanic (up from 15 percent in 2008), 15 percent black (up from 13 percent in 2008), 9.6 percent Asian (up from 5.3 percent in 2008), and 2 percent Native Americans (up from 1.6 percent in 2008). During the same timeframe, the percentage of Americans who are white will drop from 66 percent in 2008 to 46 percent in 2050 (156). As a result of these population trends, the future well-being of the United States will hinge upon the ability of Americans to accommodate, appreciate, and capitalize on its domestic diversity.

Developing an Action Plan for Infusing Diversity into Your College Experience

You increase the power of a liberal arts education and its positive impact on your personal development and career success by planning to infuse diversity into your college experience. Following is a list of specific strategies for doing so.

Incorporate diversity into your planned schedule of courses. Plan to take diversity-related liberal arts courses in your major field or as electives.

(See Exercise 2.1 at the end of this chapter to develop a systematic plan for infusing key dimensions of diversity into your college coursework.)

Be ready to consider the implications of diversity for any topic you are discussing in class or researching for course assignments. For instance, use multicultural or international examples as evidence to support and illustrate your points. If you have a choice about a research topic, consider choosing a topic that relates to diversity or has implications for diversity. (To keep abreast of current international developments for possible use in class discussions and course assignments, consult the International News Network at http://www.onlinenews.com.pk)

Take a foreign language course. Courses that develop your ability to communicate in a different language are not only educationally beneficial, they also benefit your career development because research indicates that employers seek college graduates with foreign language skills (59, 122, 22).

If possible, participate in a study-abroad or travel-study program that allows you to live in another country and to interact directly with its native citizens. In addition to coursework, you can gain an international knowledge and a more global perspective by participating in a program that enables you to actually *experience* a different country. You can do this for a full term or, perhaps, for a shorter time period (e.g., January, May, or summer term). In preparation for this international experience, take a course in the language, culture, or history of the nation to which you will be traveling. Research on students who study abroad indicates that this experience increases their perspective on the world; for example, study abroad promotes greater appreciation of international and cross-cultural differences, greater interest in world affairs, and greater commitment to peace and international cooperation (80). Furthermore, research shows that study abroad also benefits students on a personal level; for example, they develop greater self-confidence, independence, and ability to function in complex environments (35).

Engage in co-curricular experiences that involve diversity. Review your student handbook to find co-curricular programs, student activities, student clubs and organizations that emphasize diversity awareness and appreciation. Studies indicate that participation in diversity-related programs promotes critical thinking (127) and reduces unconscious prejudice (20).

Engage in volunteer experiences that allow you to work in diverse communities or neighborhoods. Studies show that people who periodically devote time to doing good things for others report higher levels of personal "happiness" or personal

> "Empirical evidence shows that the actual effects on student development of emphasizing diversity and of student participation in diversity activities are overwhelmingly positive."
> –Alexander Astin, *What Matters in College*

> "Second language study opens the door for native speakers to view their own language in perspective, to understand their own culture from another point of view. This enhanced perspective allows a greater appreciation not only of English vocabulary and language usage but of the American cultural tradition and its values."
> –David Conley, author, *College Knowledge*

"I remember
that my self-
image was being
influenced by the
media. I got the
impression that
women had to
look a certain
way. I dyed my
hair, wore differ-
ent clothes, more
makeup ...all be-
cause magazines,
TV, [and] music
videos 'said' that
was beautiful.
Luckily, when I
was fifteen,
I went to Brazil
and saw a differ-
ent, more natural
beauty and came
back to America
more as myself.
I let go of the hold
the media image
had on me."
—Leilani, first-year
college student

*"Intercultural
effectiveness
includes knowledge
of cultures and
cultural practices
(one's own and
others), complex
cognitive skills for
decision making
in intercultural
contexts, social
skills to function
effectively in diverse
groups and personal
attributes that
include flexibility
and openness to
new ideas."*
–Wabash National
Study of Liberal Arts
Education (2007)

satisfaction with their life (106). This is probably due to feelings of self-satisfaction and pride that come from knowing they are making a difference in someone else's life. Volunteer experiences in communities beyond the borders of your campus give you the opportunity to interact with diverse groups of people who may not be well represented in your campus community.

Volunteering also enables you to acquire hands-on work experience in "real-life" settings. You can use your volunteer opportunities to strengthen your resume and to network with professionals outside of college who may serve as excellent resources, references, and sources for letters of recommendation. Moreover, volunteer experiences can serve as "exploratory internships" by giving you the opportunity to gain diversity experience while, at the same time, allowing you to explore the world of work and gain inside information on career fields that may interest you.

Attempt to find an *internship* in a company or organization that will allow you the opportunity to work with people from diverse backgrounds and cultures. Hands-on experience with diversity not only promotes learning, it also promotes your career prospects by strengthening your preparation and qualifications for career entry after college. Whatever career you may choose to pursue, you will likely find yourself working with employers, employees, co-workers, customers, and clients from diverse cultural backgrounds because America's workforce is now more diverse than at any other time in the nation's history (and will grow ever more diverse in the future).

National surveys of policymakers, business leaders, and employers reveal that they are interested in college graduates who are more than just "aware" or "tolerant" of diversity; they want graduates who have direct, "hands on" experience with diversity (53). National surveys of American voters reveal that the overwhelming majority of them agree that diversity education helps students to learn practical skills that are essential for success in today's world—such as communication, teamwork, and problem solving. Almost one-half of voters also thought that the American education system should "put more emphasis on teaching people about each others' cultures, backgrounds, and lifestyles" (114). Thus, both employers and the American public agree that diversity education is *career preparation*.

The ability to understand, appreciate, and communicate in different cultural contexts, known as *intercultural effectiveness* or *intercultural competence*, has become such an essential life skill that it can be considered a liberal arts skill. Like other liberating skills developed by the liberal arts, intercultural effectiveness has two powerful qualities:

1. **Transferability:** It is a portable skill that "travels well" across different contexts and situations and can be transferred (applied) across a wide variety of careers, and life roles; and

2. **Durability:** It is an enduring skill with long-lasting value that can be continually used throughout life.

Interacting and Collaborating with Members of Diverse Groups

The knowledge acquired about diverse groups and cultures from your coursework should make you feel more comfortable about initiating contact with people from those groups. Research on college students demonstrates that learning is maximized when they move beyond acquiring knowledge about diversity *vicariously*—through someone else (e.g., through lectures and readings) to learning from diversity *experientially*—through direct, personal contact with people from diverse groups (109).

Formal courses and programs can help you learn *about* diversity, whereas first-hand interaction with diverse people enables you to learn directly *from* diversity. The latter represents a significant increase in your level of involvement with diversity. The difference would be comparable to acquiring knowledge about another country by reading about it, as opposed to actually going to the country and interacting with its natives. Interpersonal contact with individuals from diverse groups takes you beyond multicultural or cross-cultural awareness to *intercultural interaction*. It transforms diversity appreciation from an attitude or belief into action and commitment.

Take advantage of the Internet to "chat" with students from diverse groups on your campus, or with students in different countries. Electronic communication may be a more convenient and comfortable way to initiate interaction with members of diverse groups with whom you have had little prior experience. After communicating with them *online*, you may gain more confidence about interacting with them *in person*.

Meet members of diverse groups through *Facebook*. You can capitalize on this electronic social networking tool to meet and interact with diverse people. Since personal information and photos are often available through the *Facebook* database, you can check for announcements of social gatherings that tend to attract students from diverse backgrounds. You may also use *Facebook* to identify campus organizations whose membership includes students from diverse racial and cultural groups.

Participate in multicultural or cross-cultural retreats sponsored by your college. A retreat setting can provide a warm and comfortable environment for getting to know diverse groups of students at a more personal level, without the usual distractions of our familiar social environment and daily routine.

Spend time at the multicultural center on your campus, join a campus club, or become a member of an organization that is devoted to diversity awareness (e.g., multicultural or international student club). Spending time in such venues will enable you to make contact with members of groups other than your own, and it sends a clear message that you value contact with people from diverse cultural backgrounds, because you have taken the initiative to seek them out on "their turf."

> Liberal arts and diversity complement one another to equip you with enduring skills for a fast-changing world.

> "Mere knowledge is not power; it is only possibility. Action is power; and its highest manifestation is when it is directed by knowledge."
>
> –Francis Bacon (1561–1626), English philosopher, lawyer, and champion of modern science

> "The mere presence of persons of other cultures and subcultures [on campus] is primarily a political achievement, not an intellectual or educational achievement. Real educational progress will be made when multiculturalism becomes interculturalism."
>
> –Patrick J. Hill, professor of interdisciplinary studies, Evergreen State College

Remember: The goal of group discussions should not be to force conformity or convergence on a single "correct" answer or position. As a responsible discussion-group member, one of your roles is to encourage others to express their positions—even if they may differ from the majority. By so doing, you promote multiple perspective-taking and balanced thinking, which are two key characteristics of critical thinkers.

Seek out the views and opinions of classmates from diverse backgrounds. For example, during or after class discussions, ask students who are members of different ethnic and racial groups if their personal experiences would support or contradict points made or positions taken in class. Research indicates that free discussions, in which diverse viewpoints are openly sought and included, is one of the most effective ways to develop critical thinking skills (88).

Join or form discussion groups with students from diverse backgrounds. Research consistently shows that we learn more from people who differ from us than we do from people similar to us (124, 127). For instance, older students often have a wider range of realistic life experiences that younger students can draw upon and learn from, while younger students may bring a fresh, idealistic perspective to group discussions that would benefit older students. Also, males and females may bring different thinking styles to your group discussions. Studies show that males are more likely to be "separate knowers"—i.e., they are more likely to "detach" themselves from the topic or issue being discussed so they can analyze it. In contrast, females are more likely to be "connected knowers"—they are more likely to relate personally to the topic and connect it to their own experiences. For example, when confronting a poem, males are more likely to ask themselves, "What techniques can I use to analyze it?" In contrast, females are more likely to ask themselves, "What is the poet trying to say to me?" (17). It has also been found that females tend to adopt a more collaborative style during group discussions and are more likely to collect ideas of others in group-learning situations. Studies also show that males are more likely to adopt a competitive approach and debate the ideas of others (99).

You can gain access to diverse perspectives by joining or forming groups of students who differ from you in terms of such characteristics as gender, age, race, or ethnicity. You could begin by forming discussion groups with students who are diverse in terms of certain physical or cultural characteristics but who have common interests or goals. For instance, you could form a study group comprised of students with the same major as you, but who differ with respect to race, ethnicity, or age. This strategy would give the diverse members of your group common ground for discussion (their shared major) and raise awareness that humans who are members of diverse groups can, at the same time, share similar interests and goals.

Reflection 2.12

How would you define teamwork? What do you think are the key characteristics of successful learning teams (e.g., study groups or group projects)?

Form collaborative learning teams with students from diverse backgrounds. A learning *team* is much more than a discussion group; it moves beyond discussion to collaboration—they "co-labor" (work together) as part of a joint and mutually-supportive effort to reach the same learning goal. Research on students from kindergarten through college clearly indicates that when they collaborate in teams, their academic performance and interpersonal skills improve significantly (46). Studies also show that when individuals from different ethnic and racial groups work collaboratively to attain a common goal, it reduces racial prejudice and promotes interracial friendships (3, 6). Scholars believe that these positive diversity-related results can be explained by the fact that when individuals from diverse groups work collaboratively on the same team, no one is a member of an "out group" (them); instead, they are all members of the same "in group" (us) (133, 144). For a summary of the characteristics of effective collaborative learning teams, see **Box 2.3**.

> Remember: Including diversity in your discussion groups not only provides social variety, it also promotes the quality of your group's thinking by enabling its members to gain access to, and learn from, people with diverse life experiences and cultural perspectives.

BOX 2.3   Tips for Teamwork: Creating Successful Collaborative Learning Groups

1. **Intentionally form diverse learning teams comprised of individuals with different cultural backgrounds and life experiences.** Research consistently shows that we learn more from people who are different from us than we do from people who are similar to us, and we learn best from others whose experiences and viewpoints do not necessarily match our own. Thus, the best learning teams to join or form are those comprised of people who are dissimilar to you, or who have characteristics that are not very familiar to you. Ideal teammates are individuals who are different than you in terms of age, gender, ethnicity, race, culture or geographic backgrounds, learning styles, and personality characteristics. Such variety brings different life experiences, styles of thinking, and learning strategies to your team, which not only serves to enrich its diversity, but its productivity as well. If you team up only with friends or classmates whose lifestyles and experiences are similar to your own, it can actually impair your team's performance. Your similar experiences can cause your learning to get off track and onto topics that have nothing to do with the learning task (for example, what you did last weekend or what you are planning to do next weekend).

2. **The team should identify a clear, common goal.** The team should work toward producing a single, unified product that represents the group's collective effort and reflects a concrete accomplishment (e.g., a completed sheet of answers to questions, a list or chart of specific ideas). Such a jointly-shared end product helps individual members function as "we" rather than "me," and helps the team stay on task and moving in the same direction–toward their common goal.

> Simply stated, studies show that we learn more from people who differ from us than us do from people who are similar to us. Ignoring or blocking out the experiences and ideas of others who are unfamiliar to us is not only a poor social skill; it's also a poor learning strategy.

3. **Each teammate should have equal opportunity and personal responsibility for contributing to the team's final product.** For example, all team members should be equally responsible for making a specific contribution to the team's final product—such as contributing a specific perspective (e.g., national, global, or ethical) or form of thinking (e.g., analysis, synthesis, or application).

4. **All teammates should work interdependently—that is, they should depend on or rely upon each other to achieve their common goal.** Similar to a sports team, each member of the collaborative learning team should have a specific role to play. For instance, each teammate could assume one of the following roles:

   - **Manager:** Whose role is to assure that the team stays on track and moving toward their goal;

   - **Moderator:** Whose role is to ensure that all members have equal opportunity to contribute,

   - **Summarizer:** Whose role is to monitor the team's progress, identifying what has been accomplished and what remains to be done; or

   - **Recorder:** Whose role Is to keep a written record of the team's ideas.

     Teammates may also assume roles that involve contributing a different perspective to the team's overall topic or project–as if each teammate were bringing a different part or piece of the puzzle that's needed to complete the whole puzzle. For example, different team members could contribute the following perspectives:

   - **Time** (e.g., past., present, or future)

   - **Place** (e.g., national, international, global)

   - **Person** (e.g., social, emotional, or physical)

5. **Before delving into the work task, teammates should allow some social "warm up" time for teammates to get to know one another and create a sense of team solidarity or group identity.** Teammates need to feel comfortable with each other as persons before they can feel comfortable about sharing their personal thoughts and viewpoints, particularly if the team is comprised of individuals from diverse (and unfamiliar) cultures. Before tackling the learning task, teammates should informally interact to learn each other's names, backgrounds, and interests.

6. **Teamwork should take place in a friendly, informal setting.** The context or atmosphere in which group work takes place can influence the nature and quality of interaction among team members. People are more likely to work openly and collaboratively when they are in an environment that is conducive to relationship building. For example, a living room or a lounge area would provide a warmer and friendlier atmosphere than a sterile classroom.

7. **Learning teams should occasionally divide into smaller subgroups (e.g., as pairs or trios) so that teammates get an opportunity to work with each other on a more personal level, particularly if they are from different ethnic or racial groups.** The smaller the group size, the greater the level of participation, involvement, and depth of interaction between group members. For example, it's hard to get lost in a group of two. If multiple opportunities are created for different team members to work together in a small group, everyone has at least one opportunity to work closely every other member of the team. This can also promote diversity appreciation by allowing each team member to experience working at a personal level with an individual from a minority (racial or ethnic group) that is not represented in large numbers on campus.

When contact between people from diverse groups takes place under the above conditions, it can have the most positive impact on learning and diversity appreciation. A win-win scenario is created: Learning is strengthened while, at the same time, prejudice is weakened.

References: (5, 4, 9, 40, 143, 162).

> *"TEAM = **T**ogether **E**veryone **A**chieves **M**ore"*
> –Author Unknown

After concluding your work in small-group discussions or collaborative learning teams, take time to pause and reflect on the group experience. Ask yourself questions that trigger personal reflection on the ideas that were shared by diverse members of your group and carefully consider the impact of those ideas on you. For instance, following group discussions you could ask yourself the following questions:

- What major similarities in viewpoints or background experiences did all group members share? (What were the themes?)
- What major differences of opinion were expressed by members of diverse groups during the discussion? (What were the variations on the theme?)
- Were there particular topics or issues raised during the discussion that provoked intense reactions or very emotional responses from members of the group?
- Did the discussion cause me to reconsider or change any position(s) I previously held?

When reflecting on your diversity experiences, consider not only the knowledge you acquired, but also their emotional impact on you. For example, ask yourself the following questions:

- What type of feelings did I experience?
- When and where did I experience these feelings? (What was the particular point or statement made that triggered these feelings?)

- Why did I experience these feelings?
- Did this experience change my attitudes or beliefs? (If yes, how? If no, why not?)

Keep a diversity *journal* for recording of your personal reflections on diversity. Learning deeply from diversity requires both action and *reflection*. Studies show that college students learn most effectively from diversity experiences when they take time to reflect on these experiences and record their reflections in writing (95, 109). Personal reflection is the natural complement and sequel to active involvement. Both processes are needed for learning to be complete and "go deep." Active involvement is necessary to initially capture and engage your *attention*— which enables you to "get into" the learning task and get information through your attention filter and into your brain. Reflection is also needed to enable you to slow down, step back and review the learning experience—which ensures that it gets "locked" deeply into your long-term memory system (28, 21).

Writing is an effective strategy for promoting reflection on any diversity experi- ence (or any learning experience) because it "forces" you to carefully and systemati- cally think through the experience; it also provides you with a visible product of your thought process that you can review later to stimulate further reflection on your experience (8, 90). The power of writing is highlighted by interviews with graduat- ing seniors who were asked to think of all the courses they have taken in college and identify "which course, or courses, had the most profound impact on you, on the way you think, about learning, about life, about the world?" When answering this question, graduating seniors were most likely to cite courses in which they had done a significant amount of writing (93).

Take a Leadership Role with Respect to Diversity

Your experiences with diversity may present an opportunity for you to demon- strate your civic character and leadership skills. Research shows that the most effec- tive leaders are those who enable diverse individuals to see themselves as members of the same group or team, and that by advancing the group's interest, they are advanc- ing their own interests (16). By embracing diversity and creating a welcoming, inclu- sive community, you demonstrate leadership. Both white students and students of color feel a greater sense of belonging when they perceive themselves as members of a college community that is open and welcoming to students from different ethnic and racial groups (94).

Serve as a community builder by identifying common themes that unite the ideas and experiences of students from varied backgrounds. Look for the common denominators—themes of unity that underlie diversity. Individuals from diverse ethnic and racial groups still share many common characteristics as a result of being citizens of the same country, persons of the same gender, or members

> By learning about diversity (our differences), we simultaneously learn more about our commonality — our shared humanity.

of the same generation. No matter what particular racial or ethnic group(s) an individual belongs to, humans of all races and ethnicities live in neighborhoods and are members of communities, develop friendships and intimate relationships, have emotional needs, pass through the stages of the human life cycle and undergo life transitions, and grapple with the universal and eternal issues of personal identity and mortality.

As you look to identify and capitalize on diversity, don't overlook the unity that characterizes our humanity—i.e., the commonalities that transcend differences and build community. Focusing exclusively on our differences without making the effort to go deeper and find the underlying similarities that lie beneath our obvious differences can intensify feelings of separation and divisiveness among diverse groups. In fact, research suggests that if diversity education focuses on differences alone, minority groups are likely to feel even more isolated (145). To minimize this marginalization of minority group members, look to build bridges of unity across islands of diversity by digging below the surface to unearth the common ground from which our differences grow.

One strategy for doing so with diverse groups of people is to *begin* discussions by first identifying what your group members have in common—before launching into any discussion of your differences. For example, before beginning a discussion of cultural differences, you might first discuss the common elements of all cultures (e.g., language, family, artistic expression, traditions). This initial identification of similarities can help defuse feelings of divisiveness and defensiveness, and provide a common ground upon which an open and authentic discussion of diversity can be built.

Keep abreast of current issues relating to prejudice and discrimination and take an active role in promoting social justice. While college is about bettering yourself, both personally and professionally, it's also about promoting the public good. As you may recall, the original purpose of a college education was to preserve our nation's freedom. As a democracy, the United States is a nation that was built on the foundation of equal rights and freedom of opportunity for all groups of people, regardless of their majority or minority status. The election process is what drives an effective democracy; by exercising your right to vote, you are preserving democracy. When you vote, be mindful of political leaders who are committed to ensuring equal rights, and social justice. When the rights or freedom of any group of citizens are threatened by prejudice and discrimination, the political stability and survival of all citizens in a democratic nation are threatened. Diversity and democracy go hand-in-hand; by appreciating the former, you preserve the latter.

To remain informed about current events relating to the preservation of social justice and prevention of human rights' violations across the nation and around the world, the following two websites are recommended.

> Raising your fellow students' awareness of the universal themes that unite diverse groups under the common umbrella of humanity reduces the risk that highlighting differences will heighten divisiveness.

> "
> *"A successful democracy demands tolerance and mutual respect from different groups within its citizenry in order to contain the religious and ethnic tensions that have driven so many countries around the world."*
> —Derek Bok, former president, Harvard University

Figure 2.5. Personal Characteristics that Provide an Effective Foundation for Choice of a College Major.

- **www.tolerance.org** This is the site of an educational and public service organization for people interested in fighting bigotry in America and creating communities that value diversity. It tracks hate groups, hate crimes, hate Web sites, and hate music. It also supplies research-based strategies for promoting social justice on campuses and in the community. You can subscribe to a free newsletter that provides updates on the latest social, educational, and legal news relating to diversity and bigotry.

- **www.amnesty.org** This is the Web site of Amnesty International (AI)—which is a worldwide organization of people committed to preserving human rights. While Tolerance.org is a national organization, AI is an international movement that includes almost two million members from over 150 countries in every region of the world. Many of these people have very different political and religious beliefs, but they share the common concern and goal: to prevent violation of human rights. Its Web site includes strategies for protecting and promoting human rights, as well as information on how to join the organization and participate in its local volunteer activities.

If you visit this site, read AI's *Universal Declaration of Human Rights*—a powerful document that has been translated into more than 300 different languages for worldwide use.

Take a stand against prejudice on campus by constructively disagreeing with those who make stereotypical statements or prejudicial remarks. Studies show that when members of the same group observe another group member make prejudicial remarks, the group's prejudice tends to increase—probably due the pressure of group conformity (146). In contrast, if a group member's prejudicial comment is challenged by another member of his or her own group, particularly a fellow member who is liked and respected, the person's prejudice tends to decrease, as does any prejudice held by other members of the group (15). Thus, by taking a leadership role and challenging someone from your own group who makes prejudicial remarks, you not only help reduce that person's prejudice, you reduce prejudice among others who witness your challenge.

By being open to diversity and actively opposing prejudice, you demonstrate civic character. You become a role model whose actions visibly demonstrate to other student citizens in your college community that diversity has both educational and ethical value. You show others that appreciating diversity is not only a *smart* thing to do; it's also the *right* thing to do.

Journal Entry 2.1

How would you interpret the meaning or message of the following quotes?

"Every human is, at the same time, like all other humans, like some humans, and like no other human."

—Clyde Kluckholn, American anthropologist

"The more eyes, different eyes, we can use to observe one thing, the more complete will our concept of this thing, our objectivity, be."

—Friedrich Nietzsche, German philosopher

"The mere presence of persons of other cultures and subcultures [on campus] is primarily a political achievement, not an intellectual or educational achievement. Real educational progress will be made when multiculturalism becomes inter-culturalism."

—Patrick J. Hill, Professor of interdisciplinary studies, Evergreen State College

Journal Entry 2.2

Racial bias can be subtle and may only begin to surface when the social distance between members of different groups grows closer.

Rate your level of comfort (high, medium, or low) in the following interracial social situations.

1.	Going to your school	high	medium	low
2.	Working in your place of employment	high	medium	low
3.	Living on your street as a neighbor	high	medium	low
4.	Living with you as a roommate	high	medium	low
5.	Socializing with you as a personal friend	high	medium	low
6.	Being your most intimate friend or romantic partner	high	medium	low
7.	Being your partner in marriage	high	medium	low

For the item(s) you rated "high," why would you feel comfortable?

For the item(s) you rated "low," why would you feel uncomfortable?

Journal Entry 2.3

We can be members of multiple groups at the same time and our membership in these overlapping groups likely has influenced our personal development and identity. In the following figure, consider the shaded center circle to be yourself and the six non-shaded circles to be six different groups that you are a member of and that you think have influenced your personal development or personal identity.

Fill in the non-shaded circles with the names of groups to which you belong that have had the most influence on your personal development and identity. You can use the diversity spectrum that appears on page 33 of this chapter to help you identify different groups to which you may belong. Don't feel you have to come up with six groups to fill all six circles. What is more important is to identify those groups that have had a significant influence on your personal development or identity.

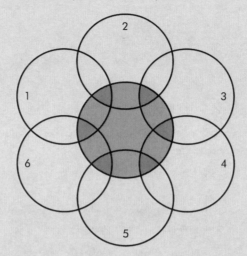

After you identify these groups, take a moment to reflect on the following questions:

1. Which one of your groups has had the greatest influence on your personal development and identity? Why?

2. Have you ever felt limited or disadvantaged by being a member of any your group(s)? Why?

3. Have you ever felt that you experienced advantages or privileges because of your membership in any group(s)? Why?

Journal Entry 2.4

If you were to be born again as a member of a different racial or ethnic group:

What group would you want it to be? Why?

With your new group identity, what aspects of your life do you think would likely change the most? Why?

Despite your new group identity, what aspects of your life do you think would likely remain the same? Why?

(Adapted from the University of New Hampshire, Office of Residential Life, 2001, 153).

Journal Entry 2.4

Reflect on your responses to the reflection questions in this chapter. Which one(s) do you find to be most personally significant or revealing? Why?

Exercise 2.1 Developing an Educational Plan for Making the Most of Diversity

By planning to infuse diversity into your college experience, you increase the power of the liberal arts by further broadening its multiple perspectives and adding to its repertoire of transferable, lifelong skills.

Review your catalogue and identify diversity-related courses that you could take in each of the three key areas of college coursework: general education, your college major (or possible major), and your free electives. Use the form below to note these courses.

General Education Courses See your college *catalogue* or *bulletin* for general education requirements. (If you completed the general education plan on p. 29, see if any of those courses could also be listed here as addressing a dimension of diversity.)	Dimension of Diversity Developed by This Course See the *Diversity Spectrum* on p. 33 for a listing of different dimensions of diversity. Be sure to list at least one course that relates to cultural diversity within the U.S. (domestic diversity) and one that relates to cultural diversity across different nations (international diversity).
Requirements for Your College Major (Or a Major that You Are Considering)	**Dimension of Diversity Developed by This Course**
Free Electives (Not Required for General Education or Your Major)	**Dimension of Diversity Developed by This Course**

CHAPTER 3

The Benefits of Experiencing the Liberal Arts and Diversity

Reflection 3.1

Before you begin reading this chapter, please answer the following question: Based on what you have read thus far in this book, what would you say is the major benefit of experiencing:

    1. The liberal arts?

    2. Diversity?

This chapter is designed to pull together all the key benefits of experiencing a college education infused with the liberal arts and diversity. By becoming aware of these benefits, you should become more motivated to acquire them and better able to articulate them. Potential employers, graduate schools, and professional schools are more often interested in what specific qualities and skills you have acquired than what courses you took or what your major was. Thus, by intentionally planning for and tracking the key skills and perspectives developed by the liberal arts and diversity, you become more aware of them, more likely to use them, and better able to communicate them to others.

Twelve key benefits (positive outcomes) of experiencing the liberal arts and diversity will be discussed in this chapter:

1. Gaining greater self-knowledge, self-awareness and self-insight.

2. Learning more effectively and efficiently.

3. Acquiring mental flexibility and ability to be a lifelong learner.

4. Thinking critically from multiple perspectives.

5. Thinking creatively.

6. Promoting exploration and direction for choice of a college major.

7. Acquiring skills for success in your college major.

8. Preparing for career entry.

9. Diversifying career options and increasing career versatility.

10. Strengthening prospects for career advancement and leadership.

11. Widening personal interests and strengthening social self-confidence.

12. Preparing for multiple life roles and responsibilities beyond college.

Remember: You shouldn't build your personal identity around a major and a career; you build your major and career around your personal identity.

The more opportunities you create to learn from people whose cultures differ from your own, the more opportunities you create to learn about yourself.

◆ Gaining Greater Self-Knowledge, Self-Awareness and Self-Insight

As mentioned in the first chapter of this book, one of the most frequently-cited educational outcomes of the liberal arts is to "know thyself" (44). The ability to turn inward and introspect (to inspect or examine yourself) is considered to be one major form of human intelligence, known as "intrapersonal intelligence" (63).

Self-awareness also represents the critical first step in making decisions about your future, including your major, your career, and all other significant life choices. You need to know yourself well before you can know choices are best for you. While this may seem obvious, self-awareness and self-discovery are often overlooked aspects of the decision-making process. Being true to yourself is critical for students first involved in making any important choice in life.

The wide range of courses and questions that you are exposed to in the liberal arts will help you become more deeply aware of different dimensions of yourself, including those that are essential for making effective major and career decisions, such as:

Your interests: What you like doing.

Your talents: What you do well.

Your values: What you believe is right or most important to do.

Know Thyself

Self-awareness is one of the most important outcomes of a liberal arts education.

Experiencing diversity further facilitates and deepens your self-awareness. Interacting with people from diverse backgrounds serves to sharpen your self-knowledge and self-insight by enabling you to compare and contrast your life experiences with others whose experiences differ sharply from your own. When you see yourself in relation to other people and other times, you acquire a reflective mirror that allows you to look at yourself from a different perspective—a *comparative perspective* that supplies you with a reference point for seeing more clearly how your particular cultural background has shaped your personal beliefs, values, and lifestyle.

When students across the United States were interviewed about their diversity experiences in college, many reported that these experiences enabled them to learn more about themselves. Some said that their interactions with students from different races and ethnic groups produced "unexpected" or "jarring" self-insights (93).

Furthermore, gaining greater self-awareness though diversity experiences is the first step to overcoming personal biases that underlie prejudice and block appreciation of diversity. By contrasting our experiences with others from diverse backgrounds, we see what is distinctive about ourselves and how we may be uniquely advantaged or disadvantaged relative to others. For instance, by seeing what limited opportunities there are for people to attend college in many other countries today, and by seeing what limited opportunities there were for certain groups of people in our own country not too long ago, we become instantly aware that the educational opportunities that Americans have today to attend college and advance themselves—regardless of their race, gender, age, or prior academic record—is truly a unique opportunity that should neither be overlooked nor underestimated.

Acquiring the Ability to Learn More Effectively (Deeply) and Efficiently

Learning occurs when your brain develops a physical (neurological) connection between the new concept you are trying to learn and something you already know that is stored in your brain (see **Figure 3.1**). The wide variety of thinking styles and the broad base of knowledge developed by the liberal arts increases the number and variety of learned connections your brain makes (e.g., knowledge and skills learned from the variety of liberal arts disciplines), creating more pathways it has to build on and connect new ideas to, which accelerates and deepens your learning. This serves to accelerate your "learning curve," enabling you to continue to learn more efficiently and effectively.

Experiencing diversity also deepens learning because when we encounter something unfamiliar, we have to stretch beyond our "mental comfort zone" and work harder to understand it. The only way to learn something new or different is by making the extra mental effort to compare and contrast it to what we

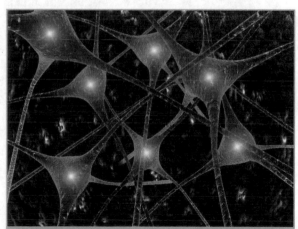

© Jurgen Ziewe, 2010 Under license from Shutterstock, Inc.

Figure 3.1 Learning derives from the latin root "lira," meaning furrow or track. When we learn, a neurological track or path is created in our brain that connects what we are trying to learn to what we already know. When a variety or multiplicity of connections have already been made in the brain, the more "hooks" there are available on which new ideas can be connected (learned). This enables learning to occur more rapidly and become more deeply rooted.

already know (1, 108). The expenditure of additional psychological energy to make this mental "stretch" serves to strengthen and deepen learning. Research consistently shows that we learn more from people who are different from us than we do from people who are similar to us (124, 127).

Reflection 3.2

What do you think is the key difference between acquiring factual knowledge versus a transferable skill?

Acquiring Mental Flexibility and Ability to Learn Throughout Life

There is a major difference between learning factual knowledge and learning transferable skills. The transferable skills developed by the liberal arts, such as communication skills and critical thinking, are "portable"; they can be carried with you and applied to different academic subjects, different career positions, and different life roles beyond college. It could be said that these transferable learning skills are the equivalent of a mental "gift that keeps on giving."

Five major types of transferable skills developed by the liberal arts are summarized in **Box 3.1**.

As you read them, rate yourself on each skill using the following scale:

4 = very strong

3 = strong

2 = needs some improvement

1 = needs much improvement

> "If you give a man a fish, you feed him for a day.
> If you teach a man how to fish, you feed him for life."
> –Author unknown

BOX 3.1 Transferable, Lifelong-Learning Skills Developed by the Liberal Arts

One way the liberal arts "liberate" you is by equipping you with skills that are not tied to any particular subject area or career field, but which can be transferred freely to different learning situations and contexts throughout life. Some key forms of these versatile, durable skills are listed below.

1. **Communication Skills:** Accurate *comprehension* and articulate *expression* of ideas. Two particular types of communication skills are essential for success in any specialized academic or career field:

   - **Written Communication Skills:** Writing in a clear, creative, and persuasive manner.
   - **Oral Communication Skills:** Speaking in a concise, confident, and eloquent fashion.

2. **Information Processing Skills**
   - **Reading Skills:** Comprehending, interpreting, and evaluating the literal and symbolic meaning of written words that are expressed in a variety of styles and subject areas.
   - **Listening Skills:** Comprehending spoken words effectively and empathically.
3. **Information Literacy Skills:** Accessing, retrieving, and evaluating information from a variety of sources, including in-print and online (technology-based) systems.
4. **Quantitative Reasoning Skills:** Ability to accurately calculate, analyze, summarize, interpret, and evaluate numerical information or statistical data.
5. **Higher-Level Thinking Skills:** Thinking that involves higher levels of reasoning than merely memorizing and recalling factual information (e.g., analysis and synthesis, critical and creative thinking).

> "Ability to recognize when information is needed and the ability to locate, evaluate, and use it effectively."
> –Definition of "information literacy," American Library Association Presidential Committee on Information Literacy

Reflection 3.3

Reflect on the five key skill areas described in **Box 3.1**, and identify one that you think is the most important or most relevant to your future goals. Write a one-paragraph explanation about why you chose this skill.

In a classic work titled, *The Idea of a University*, John Henry Newman eloquently explains how a liberal arts education prepares you for any career or any major:

> *It is the education which gives a man [woman] a clear conscious view of his own opinions and judgments, a truth in developing them, an eloquence in expressing them, and a force in urging them. It teaches him to see things as they are, to go right to the point, to detect what is sophisticated, and to discard what is irrelevant. It prepares him to fill any post with credit, and to master any subject with facility (116).*

> "You know you've got to exercise your brain just like your muscles."
> –Will Rogers, humorist, actor, and Native American

To use an athletic analogy, what the liberal arts do for the mind is similar to what cross-training does for the body. Cross-training engages the body in a wide range of different exercises to promote total physical fitness and a broad set of physical skills (e.g., strength, endurance, flexibility, and agility), which can be applied to improve performance in any sport or athletic endeavor. Similarly, the liberal arts and diversity engage the mind in a wide range of subject areas (e.g., arts, sciences, and humanities) and multiple cultural perspectives, which develop a wide range of mental skills that can be used to improve performance in any major or career.

"WHEN DID THEY START USING A SEARCH ENGINE?"

A liberal arts education develops lifelong learning skills, such as the ability to access and retrieve information, which you can used to continually acquire new knowledge throughout life.

Students often see general education as something to "get out of the way" or "get behind them" so they can get into their major and career (11). Don't buy into the belief that general education represents a series of obstacles along the way to a degree. Instead, "get into" general education and take away from it a set of powerful skills, which are *portable*—that "travel" well across different work situations and life roles and *stable*—that will remain relevant across changing times and stages of life.

General education skills are particularly important for success in today's work world. The global economy has progressed from agrarian (farm-based) to industrial (machine-based) to technological (information-based). The current technological revolution is generating information and new knowledge at a faster rate than at any other time in human history (50). When new information is rapidly created and communicated, knowledge quickly becomes obsolete (110). In order to perform their jobs and advance in their careers, workers in the today's complex, fast-changing world need to continually update their skills and learn new skills (118). This need for lifelong learning creates demand for workers who have *learned how to learn*—a hallmark of the liberal arts.

◆ Thinking Critically from Multiple Perspectives

When you think critically from multiple perspectives, you view yourself and the world around you from various angles or vantage points. For example, you're able to think from the following four key vantage points:

1. Person (self)
2. Place
3. Time
4. Culture

To think from multiple perspectives enables you to understand how each of these four dimensions influences, and is influenced by, any issue you are examining or discussing. For example, you're able to ask and answer the following questions about all issues:

- How does it affect different individuals? (The Perspective of Person)
- What impact does it have on people living in different countries? (The Perspective of Place)
- How will future generations of people be affected by this issue? (The Perspective of Time)
- How is this issue likely to be interpreted or experienced by groups of people who share different social customs and traditions? (The Perspective of Culture)

Important world issues, problems, and challenges do not exist in isolation, but as parts of an interconnected, multiple-perspective system. For example, the current issue of global warming involves the earth's atmosphere gradually thickening and trapping more heat—which has been attributed to a collection of greenhouse gases

> "In times of change, learners inherit the earth . . . [they] find themselves beautifully equipped to deal with a world that no longer exists."
> –Eric Hoffer, author of *The Ordeal of Change* and recipient of the Presidential Medal of Freedom

> "The only person who is educated is the one who has learned how to learn and change."
> –Carl Rogers, influential humanistic psychologist and Nobel Peace Prize nominee

that are being produced primarily by the burning of fossil fuels. It's theorized that this increase of man-made pollution is causing temperatures to rise (and sometimes fall) around the world, contributing to natural disasters such as droughts, wildfires, and dust storms (113, 77).

To fully understand and address the issue of global warming involves the ability to take the perspective of multiples fields of study, which include:

Ecology: Understanding the interrelationship between humans and their natural environment;

Physical science: The need for research and development of alternative sources of energy;

Economics: Minimizing expenses or creating economic incentives for industries to change their existing sources of energy;

National politics: Laws may need to be created to encourage or enforce changes in industry's use of energy sources; and

International relation: Collaboration will need to take place among all countries that are currently contributing to the problem and could contribute to its future solution.

Thus, a comprehensive understanding and solution to the issue of this global problem also involves interrelationships among the following perspectives developed by the liberal arts (see in **Figure 3.2**).

Reflection 3.4

Briefly explain how the perspectives of person, place, time, and culture may be involved in causing and solving one the following problems:

1. War and terrorism;
2. Poverty and hunger;
3. Prejudice and discrimination;
4. Developing sustainable energy; or
5. Any world issue of your choice.

Reaching accurate conclusions and making effective decisions requires use of what some scholars call "systems thinking"—taking into account how our decisions affect and are affected by other parts of a larger, interrelated system (141). The concept of systems thinking underscores the importance of viewing issues from multiple perspectives—such as those included in the lists that you have just read. It is unlikely that all perspectives on these lists will be equally involved in each issue you study; thus, it may be best to use the four lists of perspectives as checklists. Scan them to check for perspectives that relate to any issue you're examining, and use them to identify whether any relevant perspectives may have been overlooked in your thinking or in the thinking of others.

STUDENT PERSPECTIVE

"To me, thinking at a higher level is when you approach a question or topic thoughtfully [and] when you fully explore every aspect of that topic from all angles."

–First-year college student

One's reality is not everyone's reality; our current perceptions of the external world are shaped (and sometime distorted) by our prior cultural experiences. When you step outside of your own culture and view issues from a broader "world view," you're able to perceive "reality" and evaluate "truth" from diverse vantage points. This makes your thinking more comprehensive and less ethnocentric (centered on your own culture).

Perspective	Implication
Person	Global warming involves us on an individual level because our personal efforts at energy conservation in our homes and our willingness to purchase energy-efficient products can play a major role in solving this problem.
Place	Global warming is an international issue that extends beyond the boundaries of one's own country to all countries in the world, and its solution will require worldwide collaboration.
Time	If the current trend toward higher global temperatures caused by global warming continues, it could seriously threaten the lives of future generations of people who inhabit our planet.
Culture	The problem of global warming has been caused by industries in technologically advanced cultures, yet the problem of rising global temperatures is likely to have its most negative impact on less technologically advanced cultures that lack the resources to respond to it (Joint Science Academies Statement, 2005). To prevent this from happening, technologically advanced cultures will need to use their advanced technology to devise alternative methods for generating energy that does not continue to release heat-trapping gases into the atmosphere.

Figure 3.2 Perspective/implications.

Experiencing diversity further expands the multiplicity of perspectives from which you can understand and solve problems. Just as exposure to a diversity of disciplines in the liberal arts curriculum opens your mind to multiple perspectives, so too does exposure to the diversity of human cultures. Cultural and disciplinary diversity work together to liberate you from narrowness; they empower you to view yourself and the world around you from a wide variety of perspectives.

A major advantage of culture is that it helps bind its members together into a supportive, tight-knit community; however, it can also blind its members from taking other cultural perspectives. Since culture shapes the way we think, it can cause groups of people to view the world solely through their own cultural lens or frame of reference (37). Viewing the world from one cultural perspective provides a one-dimensional, incomplete understanding of any issue because it represents a one-sided (ethnocentric) viewpoint that reflects the biased perspective of one particular vantage point (54).

Optical illusions are a good illustration of how our cultural perspectives can bias us, and lead to inaccurate perceptions. For instance, compare the length of the two lines in **Figure 3.3**.

If you perceive the line on the right to be longer than the line on the left, welcome to the club. Virtually all Americans and people from Western cultures perceive the line on the right to be longer. Actually, both lines are equal in length. (If you don't believe it, take out a ruler and check it out.) Interestingly, this perceptual error is not made by people from non-Western cultures living in environments populated with circular structures (see the picture below), rather than structures with straight lines and angled corners, like the rectangular houses and buildings that characterize Western cultures (140).

The key point underlying this optical illusion is that our cultural experiences that are stored in

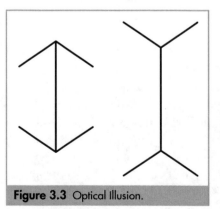

Figure 3.3 Optical Illusion.

our brain shape and sometimes distort our perceptions of reality. We think we are seeing things objectively or as they really are, but we are often seeing things subjectively from our limited cultural vantage point. Being open to the viewpoints of diverse people who perceive the world from different cultural vantage points serves to widen our range of perception and helps us overcome our "cultural blind spots." As a result, we tend to perceive the world around us with greater clarity and accuracy.

The people who live in these circular huts would not be fooled by the optical illusion in Figure 3.3.

© JupiterImages Corporation.

Diversity magnifies the power of the liberal arts by liberating us from the tunnel vision of ethnocentrism (culture-centeredness), enabling us to get beyond ourselves and our own culture to see ourselves in relation to people with different cultural backgrounds. Just as the various subject areas you experience in the liberal arts curriculum opens your mind to multiple perspectives, so do experiences with people from varied backgrounds. These experiences equip us with a wide-focus lens that allows us to take a broader, multicultural, or cross-cultural perspective. This wider perspective helps us become aware of our cultural "blind spots" and reduces the risk of *group think*—the tendency for tight, like-minded groups of people to think so much alike that they overlook flaws in their own thinking, which can lead to poor choices and faulty decisions (76).

Research on students who experience high levels of exposure to different dimensions of diversity in college (e.g., participate in multicultural courses and events on campus, and interact and form friendships with peers of different ethnic backgrounds) indicate that these students report the greatest gains in

- **Thinking complexity:** The ability to think about all parts and all sides of an issue (68);

- **Reflective thinking:** The ability to think deeply about personal and global issues (83); and

- **Critical thinking:** The ability to judge the validity of reasoning used by oneself and others (125).

Thus, experiencing diversity encourages thinking that is more nuanced and complete; it enables you to detect the variety and subtlety of factors embedded within intricate issues or dilemmas, and to detect biases in your own thinking and in the thinking of others.

Lastly, multiple-perspective thinking also reduces the likelihood of prejudice and discrimination. Racial, ethnic, and national prejudices often stem from narrow,

> "It is difficult to see the picture when you are inside the frame."
>
> —As an old saying (author unknown)

> "When all men think alike, no one thinks very much."
>
> —Walter Lippmann, distinguished journalist, and originator of the term, "stereotype"

"
"The more eyes, different eyes, we can use to observe one thing, the more complete will our concept of this thing, our objectivity, be."
–Friedrich Nietzsche, German philosopher

"
"I would go to the library and borrow scores by all those great composers, like Stravinsky, Alban Berg, Prokofiev. I wanted to see what was going on in all of music. Knowledge is freedom and ignorance is slavery . . ."
–Miles Davis, one of the most influential musicians of the twentieth century who contributed to such innovative forms of jazz music as, hard bop, cool jazz, free jazz, and fusion

self-centered, and group-centered thinking (128). Oversimplified, dualistic (either-or) thinking and biased thinking increase the risk that individuals will categorize people into in-groups ("us") or out-groups ("them"). This type of dualistic (either-or) thinking can lead, in turn, to ethnocentrism—the tendency to view one's own racial or ethnic group as the superior "in-group," while viewing other groups as inferior "out-groups." The ability to think from multiple perspectives counteracts this type of dualistic, ethnocentric thinking and, in so doing, serves as a safeguard against bias, prejudice, and discrimination.

Creative Thinking

The diversity of disciplines and viewpoints you experience in the liberal arts strengthen your ability to think *creatively*. You acquire thinking styles and strategies that can be adapted and used to create solutions to problems in a wide range of contexts or situations. Research on creative individuals reveals that they typically have a wide range of knowledge and interests, and the products of their creative thinking often reflect combinations of ideas drawn from multiple subject areas (135). Thus, creativity often emerges from a broad base of knowledge that goes beyond the boundaries of one specialized academic or professional area. Breadth of knowledge allows creative people to see relationships and make unique, combinatorial connections that involve diverse subject areas and skill sets (14, 79).

Experiencing diversity also contributes to creativity by allowing you to draw on ideas from people of diverse backgrounds and bouncing your ideas off them can generate energy, synergy, and serendipity—i.e., unexpected discoveries and creative insights. Diversity experiences will also supply you with greater breadth of knowledge and range of thinking styles that can enhance creativity by empowering you to think outside the box or boundaries of a single cultural framework. Diversity expands your capacity to view issues and problems from *multiple* cultural perspectives and vantage points, which works to your advantage when you encounter unfamiliar problems in different contexts and circumstances. In contrast, limiting your experiences with diversity limits your creativity by narrowing your range of cultural vantage points, which reduces the variety lenses you can use to view issues and solve problems.

Once diverse perspectives have been acquired, they can also be combined or rearranged in ways that result in unique or innovative solutions to problems. The ideas you acquire from diverse people and diverse cultures can complement or cross-fertilize each other, giving birth to new ideas and strategies for solving old problems. Research suggests that when ideas are generated freely in groups comprised of people from diverse backgrounds, powerful "cross-stimulation" effects occur, whereby one group member's idea often triggers creative thinking and production of new ideas from other group members (30).

Creative thinking skills fostered by the liberal arts and diversity are particularly relevant for entry and advancement in today's careers. Current employers place high value on innovative thinking skills; they are looking to hire college graduates "who can think beyond the routine and who have the ability not just to adapt to change, but to help create it" (11).

Reflection 3.5

How do you think your performance in your college major will be strengthened by your experiences with:

1. Liberal arts?
2. Diversity?

Promoting Exploration and Direction for Choice of a College Major

Reflection 3.6

Please answer the following multiple-choice question. **Note:** This not a test. (Repeat: This is not a test.)

Which of the following statements is/are true?

1. Less than 10 percent of beginning college students report that they know a great deal about the field that they are intending to major in.
2. As students proceed through the first year of college, they grow more uncertain about the major they chose when they began college.
3. Over two-thirds of new students change their mind about a major during their first year of college.
4. Only one in three college seniors end up majoring in the same field that they chose during their first year of college.
5. All of the above.

(For the correct answer, read the last sentence of the following paragraph.)

The benefit of experiencing the variety of courses that make up the liberal arts curriculum is that they enable you to become more aware of yourself while, at the same time, you become more aware of the variety of academic disciplines and subject areas that are available to you as possible majors. Your trip through the liberal arts curriculum will likely result in discovery of new personal interests and new options for majors, some of which may be in fields that you didn't know existed.

In fact, as a first-term student, it may be unrealistic for you to make a final decision about a college major before you have had at least some experience with the courses that comprise the liberal arts curriculum. One key benefit of experiencing the liberal arts at the start of your college experience is that it helps you to acquire the knowledge and critical thinking skills needed to make more informed choices and wiser decisions about your college major.

"All who wander are not lost."

–J. R. R. Tolkein, author, *Lord of the Rings*

"Your work is to discover your work and then with all your heart to give yourself to it."

–Buddha, a.k.a., Hindu Prince Gautama Siddharta (563–483 BC), founder of Buddhism

The wide range of fields in the liberal arts will provide the general context you need to make an informed decision about a specific major—by enabling you to see how your particular major fits into the bigger picture (i.e., you'll see how your tree is part of the larger forest.) Consider your excursion through the liberal arts curriculum as an exploratory journey during which you should be armed and ready to make three related discoveries:

1. Discovering the full range of choices for majors that are available to you.

2. Discovering where your special interests, talents, and values lie.

3. Discovering what specialized major best complements your special interests, talents, and values.

PERSONAL EXPERIENCE | Aaron Thompson

Introduction to Sociology and Marriage and Family were two courses I initially took to fulfill general education requirements in college. However, both courses ended up having much larger, long-term effects on my life. Sociology proved so interesting to me that it became my major and I went on to earn a PhD in the field. The Marriage and Family course intrigued me so much that I went on to conduct research and write two books on the topic. Looking back, I would have never expected that those two courses—which I took just to fulfill general education requirements—would have such a significant impact on my educational goals and future profession. Moral of this story: Don't think of liberal arts courses as a burden or a waste of time. They can do more than fulfill general education requirements. If you keep an open mind and are willing to learn, the liberal arts can have a dramatic and productive effect on your life choice.

Keep in mind that most college majors do not lead directly to a specific career. Majors that do lead directly to specific careers are often called *pre-professional* majors; they include such fields as accounting, engineering, and nursing. However, the vast majority of other college majors do not channel you directly down one particular career path. Instead, they leave you with a variety of career options after graduation.

The career path of most college graduates does not run like a straight line directly from their major to their career. For instance, most physics majors do not become physicists, most philosophy majors do not become philosophers, most history majors do not become historians, and most English majors do not become Englishmen (or Englishwomen). It is this mistaken belief that may account for the fact that business continues to be the most popular major among college students (164). Students (and their parents) see that most college graduates are employed in business settings and think that if you want to get a job in business after graduation, you better major in business.

The truth is that the trip from your college major to your eventual career(s) is less like climbing a pole and more like climbing up a tree. As illustrated in **Figure 3.4**, you begin with the tree's trunk (the foundation provided by the liberal arts), which leads to separate limbs (choices for college majors), which, in turn, leads to different branches (different career paths or options).

Note that the different sets of branches (careers) grow from the same major limb. So, too, do different sets of careers or "career families" grow from the same major. For example,

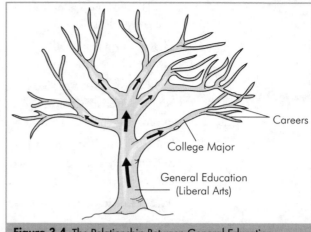

Figure 3.4 The Relationship Between General Education (Liberal Arts), College Majors, And Careers.

an English major will often lead to careers that involve use of the written language (e.g., editing, journalism, or publishing), while a major in art will often lead to careers that involve use of visual media (e.g., illustration, graphic design, or art therapy).

For most college students, choosing a major and choosing a career are not decisions made at the same time because their major doesn't turn into their career. It is this belief that leads some students to procrastinate about choosing a major; they think they're making a lifelong decision and are afraid they'll make the "wrong" choice—i.e., a choice resulting in their getting stuck doing something they hate for the rest of their life.

Acquiring Skills for Success in Your College Major

Do not assume that liberal arts courses you take as general education requirements are unrelated or irrelevant to your specialized field of interest because they a foundation for success for all college majors. Recall our story at the very start of this book about Laura, the student with a business major who questioned why she had to take a course in philosophy. Laura needed philosophy because she was going to encounter issues in her business major that involve philosophical issues, such as: (a) examining the underlying assumptions and values of capitalism relative to other economic systems (e.g., socialism), (b) business ethics (e.g., hiring and firing practices), and (c) business justice (e.g., how profits should be fairly or justly distributed to workers and shareholders). Philosophy would also strengthen her logical thinking and ethical reasoning skills so she could understand these business issues more deeply and respond to them more humanely.

Similarly, other areas of the liberal arts would provide business majors, and the many non-business majors who end up working in business organizations with

"

"A liberal education is like the Mississippi River. It has many 'distributaries' that carry its water in all directions. It meanders—going west, north, and east—before it finds its ultimate direction [and] continues to meander even once it finds its direction, but this doesn't keep it from getting to its goal."

–Dr. Richard Meadows, professor of French, Berea College and author of *The Mississippi River vs. the Erie Canal: Mapping Out the Many Advantages of a Liberal Education*

foundational knowledge and fundamental thinking skills needed to succeed in business settings. For instance:

- **History and Political Science:** Understanding governmental policies toward business laws and regulations of industry.
- **Psychology and Sociology:** Understanding how human motives and choice, both as individuals and groups, affect the productivity of workers and the purchasing habits of consumers.
- **Speech, English Composition, and Literature:** Speaking confidently and persuasively at corporate meetings, writing clear and concise memos, reading and interpreting business reports accurately and critically.
- **Mathematics:** Analyzing statistical data from marketing surveys.
- **Natural Science:** Determining effective and efficient ways to conserve energy and sustain natural resources.
- **Fine Arts:** Devising visually creative and innovative advertisements.
- **Physical and Health Education:** Selecting effective employee health-insurance plans and corporate-sponsored health services.

Beyond the field of business, the liberal arts are relevant to successful performance in all other majors and careers. For example, a historical and ethical perspective is needed in whatever any field of study or work, because all fields have a history and no field is "value free."

Although you may specialize in a particular field of study in college (your major), "real-life" issues and challenges are not neatly divided and conveniently packaged into specialized majors. Important and enduring issues, such as effective leadership, improving race relations and preventing international warfare, can neither be fully understood nor effectively solved by using the thinking tools of a single academic discipline. Approaching such important, multidimensional issues from the perspective of a single, specialized field of study would be to use a single-minded and oversimplified strategy to tackle complex and multifaceted problems.

PERSONAL EXPERIENCE | Joe Cuseo

When I decided on my major (psychology), I thought that the best thing I could do to succeed in my field was to take as many psychology courses as possible. Thus, whenever I had room in my schedule for a free elective, I would use it to take another psychology course. Looking back, I realize this was a mistake. I know now that to have a deep and complete understanding of the human mind and human behavior (two key goals of psychology) involves a broad base of knowledge that goes beyond the field of psychology. For example, it involves knowing some sociology—e.g., how group behavior and societal norms affect individual behavior; anthropology—e.g., how human cultures and their influence on human behavior have evolved over thousands of years; philosophy—e.g., how the methods used by psychology to study human behavior rest on certain assumptions or logical premises; and history—e.g., how major events in the world occurring at the time individuals are growing up can influence their attitudes, beliefs, and sources of fear. Don't make the same mistake I did. Use at least some of your electives to take liberal arts courses that broaden and deepen the knowledge you acquire in your specialized major.

> " *"The members of my senior team all graduated with a liberal arts degree, from history to political science, music to sociology. What makes them a strong team is they come from different backgrounds and are all flexible, dynamic thinkers."*
> –Alan Buckelew, CEO of Princess Cruises (158)

Preparing for Career Entry

Interviews with hundreds of employers and recent college graduates show that they both disagree that a college education should focus only on specialized knowledge and skills for a particular profession. Instead, the overwhelming majority of recent college graduates and their employers believe that the best preparation for career entry is a college education that provides career-specific preparation *plus* broad-based knowledge and general skills (129).

It is noteworthy that numerous national surveys and in-depth interviews with employers and executives in both industry and government show that the skills developed by the liberal arts are strikingly similar to the types of skills sought by employers of college graduates. These skills consistently fall into the following three categories.

> " *"When the only tool you have is a hammer, you tend to see every problem as a nail."*
> –Abraham Maslow, psychologist, best known for his theory of human self-actualization

1. **Communication skills:** Such as listening, speaking, writing, and reading (32, 111, 129).

   "There is such a heavy emphasis on effective communication in the workplace that college students who master these skills can set themselves apart from the pack when searching for employment." Marilyn Mackes, Executive Director of the National Association of Colleges and Employers (98).

2. **Thinking skills:** Such as problem solving and critical thinking (32, 129, 53).

   "We look for people who can think critically and analytically. If you can do those things, we can teach you our business." Paul Dominski, store recruiter for the Robinson-May Department Stores Company (74).

The sharp distinction often drawn between the "liberal arts" and "pre-professional" fields is a false dichotomy—an artificial divide. Both college graduates and employers of college graduates agree that a combination of general education skills and career-specific skills provide the best preparation for success in today's work world.

"They asked me during my interview why I was right for the job and I told them because I can read well, write well, and I can think. They really liked that because those were the skills they were looking for."

–English major hired by a public relations firm (Source: *Los Angeles Times*, April 4, 2004)

When you acquire lifelong learning skills, you acquire lifelong *earning* skills.

"At State Farm, our [employment] exam does not test applicants on their knowledge of finance or the insurance business, but it does require them to demonstrate critical thinking skills and the ability to calculate and think logically. These skills plus the ability to read for information, to communicate and write effectively need to be demonstrated."

–Edward B. Rust Jr., chairman and CEO, State Farm Insurance Companies (quoted in AACU, 2007)

3. **Lifelong learning skills:** Such as knowing how to learn and how to continue learning (150).

"Employers are virtually unanimous that the most important knowledge and skills the new employee can bring to the job are problem solving, communication, and 'learning to learn' skills. The workers of the future need to know how to think and how to continue to learn." David Kearns, former chief executive officer for the Xerox Corporation (81).

The remarkable resemblance between the key work skills sought by employers and the key academic skills developed by the liberal arts is not surprising when you think about the typical duties and responsibilities of working professionals. They need good communication skills to listen, speak, describe, and explain ideas to co-workers and customers. They need to read effectively in order to interpret written and statistical reports, and they need writing skills to compose numerous memos, letters, and reports. They must also possess higher-level thinking skills to analyze problems, construct well-organized plans, generate creative ideas and problem solutions, and critically evaluate whether their plans and strategies are working effectively.

While communication skills, thinking skills, and transferable learning skills rank high in importance to employers, they do not constitute the complete list of skills they seek in college graduates. Employers also place high value on the following three sets of personal characteristics.

1. **Interpersonal (Social) Skills:** Such as leadership skills, ability to collaborate, negotiate, work in teams, and relate to others with diverse characteristics and backgrounds—for example, people of different ages, races, and cultural backgrounds (32, 111, 129).

2. **Personal Qualities and Behaviors:** Such as motivation, initiative, effort, self-management, independence, personal responsibility, enthusiasm, flexibility, and self-esteem (32, 111).

3. **Personal Ethics:** Such as honesty, integrity, and ethical standards of conduct (111).

Reflection 3.7

Look at the above three categories of characteristics and note something you could do in college to begin developing each of them.

Notice that the personal characteristics and qualities sought by employers correspond closely to different elements of the "whole person" developed through general education (the curriculum and co-curriculum). Also, notice that many of the skills sought in employees are similar to the skills for liberating people to be self-directed individuals that are developed by the liberal arts (e.g., personal initiative, self-management, and individual responsibility).

The first ten years of my professional life after college were spent in corporate America. I held management and leadership roles during most of those years. As part of my job, I had the responsibility of hiring new employees and identifying the skills that most often were associated with success at the company. I identified four key skill sets and had them at the top of my list whenever I assessed new employees: (1) writing—ability to express ideas in print; (2) interpersonal skills—ability to get along well with others; (3) negotiation skills—ability to resolve conflict and bring about agreement with others; and (4) problem-solving skills—ability to identify the source of a problem and generate a solution.

If a job candidate did not have these skills, he or she could not move on to the next level of the selection process, which involved discussion of specific knowledge and technical skills relating to the position. In retrospect, the four core skills at the top of my list were among the core skills developed by general education and the liberal arts.

> "360-degree type people. That's exactly what we're looking for. Sometimes we get very technical people who are able to manage budgets and do the technical work, but their social skills just aren't very good. It's difficult to have the whole scope of talents needed."
>
> –Fairfax Business Executive (quoted in Peter D. Hart Research Associates, 2006)

Employer's Perspective

> "I look for people that take responsibility and are good team people over anything else. I can teach [them] the technical."
>
> –Milwaukee Business Executive (quoted in Peter D. Hart Research Associates, 2006)

Learning about and from diversity also prepares you for the world of work. Whatever career you may choose to pursue, you will likely find yourself working with employers, employees, co-workers, customers, and clients from diverse cultural backgrounds. America's workforce is now more diverse than at any other time in the nation's history and it will grow ever more diverse. For example, the percentage of America's working-age population who are members of minority ethnic and racial groups will jump from 34 percent in 2008 to 55 percent in 2050 (156).

In addition to the need for intercultural skills for career success in America's diverse domestic workforce, the current "global economy" places a high premium on intercultural skills relating to international diversity. The growing national and international diversity in today's work world is driving employers to seek job candidates with the following skills and attributes: sensitivity to human differences, ability to understand and relate to people from different cultural backgrounds, international knowledge, and ability to communicate in a second language (59, 111, 122, 145). Thus, learning about and from diversity is not only good education, it's good career preparation.

> "Study of the liberal arts can lead to moral understandings that are invaluable to success in whatever one attempts in life."
>
> –Peter Fellowes, president of Fellowes Manufacturing

Diversifying Career Options and Increasing Career Versatility

Another way in which the liberal arts liberate you is by freeing you from narrow job training; they empower you with flexible work skills that are applicable to a wide range of work tasks and professions. These skills increase your career freedom in three major ways: (a) freedom of career *choice*—i.e., your ability to enter different types of careers after graduating from college, (b) freedom of career *mobility*—i.e., your ability to move from one career to another, and (c) freedom of career *reentry*—i.e., your ability to move back into a career after leaving it temporarily (e.g., to raise young children).

PERSONAL EXPERIENCE | Joe Cuseo

My father is a good example of someone whose education was too narrow and whose career was too specialized. He spent approximately two years of his life learning to be a horologist—a specialist in watch and clock repair. He found regular employment for over thirty years of his working life, but then advances in technology made it possible for companies to produce and sell high-performance watches at much cheaper prices than ever before. As a result, instead of having their watches repaired when they began to malfunction, people simply threw them away and bought new ones. This reduced society's need for watch repairmen, such as my father, who soon lost his position with the watch company he was working for and was forced into early retirement.

Career versatility is particularly important in our current economy, which is being fueled by rapid advances in technology and an explosion of knowledge. Interviews with recently-hired college graduates indicate only about 50 percent of them expect to continue working in the same field in which they are currently employed (129). Follow-up studies on college graduates at later stages in their career reveal that they already have changed careers, and the further along they are in their career path, the more likely they are to be working in a field unrelated to their college major. While this may seem hard to believe, remember that the liberal arts represent a significant portion of your college education, and it is the portion that equips you with breadth of knowledge and the a variety of transferable skills (e.g., writing, speaking, thinking, information literacy). It is this broad-based knowledge and versatile set of skills that enable you to perform well in different of careers—regardless of what your particular college major happened to be.

In the current era of rapid change, existing jobs can become outdated and obsolete; at the same time, entirely new positions are emerging that never existed before (30). Nobody can be specifically trained or prepared to fill these unanticipated positions because no one knows exactly what specific knowledge and skills they will require. This growing number of unanticipated positions is creating a greater demand for *generalists* who have a broad base of knowledge, flexible lifelong-learning skills, and the mental versatility needed to handle changing work responsibilities and different professional roles (118).

While certain, specific technological skills may be "hot" right now, the demand for narrow skills tied to specific technologies, such as those relating to current computer software and Web page designs, will likely change considerably in the future. However, the demand for transferable, lifelong-learning skills needed for jobs relating to technology, such as communicating with clarity, critical thinking, creative thinking and problem solving, will remain in demand across time and changes in technology.

The demand for highly specialized work skills tends to be seasonal—they tend to come and go, like the "flavor of the month." They may be currently on the "cutting edge" but that edge will soon get frayed will need to be replaced with a new, sharper edge. The general skills provided by the liberal arts provide may not be "edgy," but they are stable and perennial; they have the durability to last longer and outlast the latest cutting edge.

◆ Career Advancement and Leadership

Studies show that as college graduates' careers progress, narrower skills learned in their major tend to decline in importance and are replaced by more general skills (127). Broader skills, such as thinking and communicating, are more important for promoting your long-term career success and your ability to move up the career ladder. Specific, specialized skills can provide you with initial job readiness (and in some careers, these specialized skills can be learned early through on-the-job training); however, the broad-based knowledge and general skills will also help you avoid the scenario of getting promoted to a professional position that you cannot perform successfully because it requires a broader set of skills than the ones you used to succeed in lower-level positions. (This scenario is sometimes referred to as the "Peter Principle"—i.e., employees within an organization will advance to their highest level of competence, then get promoted to and remain at a level at which they are incompetent.) The need for more general career skills is expected to grow even more important in the twenty-first century because the demand for upper-level positions requiring management and leadership will exceed the supply of workers available to fill these positions (71).

Reflection 3.8
Based on your experiences, what would you say are the key characteristics or qualities of people:
1. Who are interesting to talk to?
2. Who are interested in what others have to say?

> "The federal government and private organizations with extensive international interests will require the services of increasing numbers of specialists who are fluent in foreign languages and highly knowledgeable about countries, regions, and international problems."
>
> –Derek Bok, former Harvard president and author of *OurUnder-achieving Colleges*

> "The fixed person for the fixed duties, who in older societies was a blessing, in the future will be a public danger."
>
> –Alfred North Whitehead, English mathematician and philosopher

Expanding Personal Interests and Social Self-Confidence

The wider range of knowledge and skills you acquire through the liberal arts serve to expand your sphere of interests and your sources of mental stimulation. Studies show that people with a broad base of knowledge and a wide range of interests are less likely to experience boredom (67).

By broadening your perspectives and range of knowledge, you also gain greater social self-confidence. Studies show that as college students gain more general knowledge, they attain higher levels of self-esteem and social self-confidence (126, 127). Your experiences with the liberal arts will enable you to relate to people with a wider variety of educational, personal, and professional interests. You're less likely to be left out of any conversation because your broader base of knowledge allows you to feel comfortable talking about a wide variety of topics. Simply stated, you become a more interesting and interested person.

Your experiences with diversity will also promote your social development. By interacting with others from diverse backgrounds, you increase your social self-confidence in general and your ability to interact with people in a wide variety of social situations or contexts (104). Thus, seeking diversity in your social interactions serves to stimulate the development of your social skills and allows you to live a more stimulating social life. Research shows that college students who have more diversity experiences on campus report higher levels of satisfaction with their college experience (12).

Preparing for Multiple Life Roles and Responsibilities

National survey results reveal that the primary reason why students go to college today is to "prepare for a career" and "get a better job" (139). While financial security is important and work is a key element of a person's life, it is just one dimension of the total self. Our occupational role represents one of a wide variety of important roles we assume in life, which include being a family member, friend, co-worker, community member, citizen, and, possibly, mother or father. The breadth of knowledge and the versatile skills you acquire through the liberal arts will promote your ability to successfully accommodate a variety of other roles and responsibilities in life, which include, but go beyond, your career role and responsibilities. This is illustrated in the following story.

PERSONAL EXPERIENCE | *Joe Cuseo*

One life role that the liberal arts helped prepare me to fulfill was the role of father. Courses that I took in psychology and human development proved very useful in helping me understand how children develop and how a parent can best support them at different stages of their development. Surprisingly, there was another course that helped me in my parental role that I never expected.

That course was statistics, which I took to fulfill a general education requirement in mathematics. It was not a particularly enjoyable course; in fact, some of my classmates sarcastically referred to it as "sadistics" because it was not the most enjoyable experience. However, what I learned in that course turned out to be very valuable to me many years later when my 14-year-old son Tony developed leukemia—a life-threatening form of cancer that attacks healthy blood cells. Tony's type of leukemia was particularly perilous because it had only a 35 percent average cure rate; in other words, about two of every three people who developed the disease did not recover from it and eventually died. This statistic was based on patients that received the traditional treatment of chemotherapy, which was the type of treatment that my son began receiving when his cancer was first detected.

Another option for treating Tony's cancer was a bone-marrow transplant, which involved using radiation to destroy all of his own bone marrow (which was producing the cancerous blood cells) and replace it with bone-marrow donated to him by another person. My wife and I got opinions from respected doctors at two major cancer centers—one from a center that specialized in chemotherapy, and one from a center that specialized in bone-marrow transplants. The chemotherapy doctors felt strongly that drug treatment would be the better way to treat and cure Tony, and the bone-marrow transplant doctors felt strongly that his chances of survival would be much better if he had a transplant. So, my wife and I had to decide between two opposing recommendations, each made by a different group of highly regarded doctors.

To help us reach a decision, I asked both teams of doctors for research studies that had been done on the effectiveness of chemotherapy and bone-marrow transplants for treating my son's particular type of cancer. I read all of these studies and carefully analyzed their statistical findings. I remembered from my statistics course that when an "average" is calculated for a general group of people (for example, average cure rate for people with leukemia), it tends to "lump together" individuals from different subgroups (for example, males and females, young children, teenagers, and adults). Sometimes, when separate statistics are calculated for different subgroups, the results may be different than the average statistic for the whole group. So, when I read the research reports, I looked to find any subgroup statistics that may have been calculated and embedded in the reports. I found two subgroups of patients with my son's particular form of cancer that had a higher rate of cure with chemotherapy than the general (whole-group) average of 35 percent. One subgroup included people with a low number of abnormal cells at the time when the cancer was first diagnosed, and the other subgroup consisted of people whose cancer cells dropped rapidly after their first week of chemotherapy. My son belonged to both of these subgroups, which

(continued)

The liberal arts provide you with multiple set of versatile skills that enable you to do jobs that you haven't done before and jobs that haven't existed before.

While the need for specialized skills may fluctuate with supply and demand, the lifelong-learning skills developed by the liberal arts are neither trendy nor time-bound; they're able to withstand the test of time and their value is timeless.

"Employers do not want 'toothpick' graduates who have learned only the technical skills and who arrive in the workplace deep but narrow. These workers are sidelined early, employers report, because they cannot break out of their mental cubicles."
–Association of American Colleges and Universities (2007).

meant that his chance for cure with chemotherapy was higher than the overall 35 percent average. Furthermore, I found that the statistics showing higher success rate for bone-marrow transplants were based only on patients whose bodies accepted the donor's bone marrow; it did not include patients who died because their body "rejected" the donor's bone marrow. So, the success rates for bone-marrow patients were not actually as high as they appeared to be, because the overall average didn't include the subgroup of patients who died because of transplant rejection. Based on these statistics, rather than have a transplant operation, my wife and I decided to have our son treated with chemotherapy.

Our son has now been cancer-free for over five years, so we think we made the right decision. However, not in my wildest dreams could I ever imagine that a statistics course—taken many years ago to fulfill a general education requirement—would be relevant to my role as parent and help make a life-or-death decision about my own son.

BOX 3.2   Tying It Altogether: The Wide-Ranging and Long-Lasting Benefits of a College Education

When the life of college graduates (from all majors) are compared with individuals from similar social and economic backgrounds who did not continue their education beyond high school, research reveals dramatically that college graduates experience multiple, life-time benefits that reflect the breadth of knowledge, whole-person development, and lifelong-learning skills developed by the liberal arts and diversity. A summary of these benefits is listed below.

1. **Advanced Intellectual Skills**
   - Greater knowledge
   - More effective problem-solving skills
   - Better ability to deal with complex and ambiguous problems
   - Greater openness to new ideas
   - More advanced levels of moral reasoning
   - Clearer sense of self-identity—i.e., greater awareness and knowledge of personal talents, interests, values, and needs
   - Greater likelihood to continue learning throughout life

2. **Social Benefits**
   - Higher social self-confidence
   - Better ability to understand and communicate with others
   - Greater popularity
   - More effective leadership skills
   - Greater marital satisfaction

3. Emotional Benefits

- Lower levels of anxiety
- Higher levels of self-esteem
- Greater sense of self-efficacy—belief of being in control of one's life
- Higher levels of psychological well-being
- Higher levels of personal happiness

4. Physical Benefits

- Better health insurance—more likely to be covered and more comprehensive coverage
- Better dietary habits
- More likely to exercise regularly
- Lower rates of obesity
- Live longer and healthier lives

5. Civic Character

- Greater interest in national issues–both social and political
- Greater knowledge of current affairs
- More likely to vote in elections
- Higher rates of participation in civic affairs and community service

6. Career Benefits

- Greater career security and stability—lower rates of unemployment
- More career versatility and mobility—more flexibility to move out of a position and into other positions
- Better prospects for career advancement—more opportunity to move up to higher professional positions
- Higher level of career interest—more likely to find their work stimulating and challenging
- More career autonomy—greater independence and opportunity to be their own boss
- Higher level of career satisfaction—more likely to enjoy their work, find their work personally fulfilling, and feel that it allows them to use their special talents
- Greater career prestige—hold higher-status positions (i.e., careers that are more desirable and highly regarded by society)

7. Economic Advantages

- Make wiser consumer choices and decisions
- Make better long-term financial investments
- Receive greater pension benefits

- Earn higher income: Individuals with a bachelor's degree now earn an average annual salary of about $50,000 per year–40 percent higher than high school graduates–whose average salary is less than $30,000 per year. When these differences are calculated over a lifetime, families headed by people holding a bachelor's degree take in about $1.6 million more than families headed by people with a high school diploma. (This gap between the earnings of high school and college graduates is expected to grow even wider in the future).

8. **Higher Quality of Life for Their Children**
    - Less likely to smoke during pregnancy
    - Provide better health care for their children
    - Spend more time with their children
    - More likely to involve their children in mentally-stimulating educational activities
    - More likely to save money for their children to go to college
    - More likely to have children who graduate from college
    - More likely to have children who attain high-status and high-paying careers

Journal Entry 3.1

How would you interpret the meaning or message of the following quotes?

"We see what is behind our eyes."

—Chinese proverb

"When the only tool you have is a hammer, you tend to see every problem as a nail."
—Abraham Maslow, psychologist, best known for his theory of human self-actualization

"Your work is to discover your work and then with all your heart to give yourself to it."
—Buddha, a.k.a., Hindu Prince Gautama Siddharta (563–483 BC), founder of Buddhism

Journal Entry 3.2

1. I would define *success* as . . . .

2. For me, a successful *career* is one that . . . .

3. For me, to lead a rewarding and fulfilling *life*, one must . . .

Journal Entry 3.3

Rank the following in terms of their importance to you (1 = highest; 4 = lowest);

___ Getting a position in a career immediately after college (career entry)

___ Moving up in a career (career advancement)

___ Being able to move from one career to another (career mobility)

___ Being able to take time off from a career and return to it later (career re-entry)

My *highest*-ranked item was chosen first because . . .

My *lowest*-ranked item was ranked last because . . .

Journal Entry 3.4

Reflect on your responses to the reflection questions in this chapter. Which one(s) do you find to be most personally significant or revealing? Why?

Exercise 3.1 Faculty Interview

Make an appointment to interview a faculty member in a field of study that interests you as a possible major or minor (or a field that you are just curious about). Following is a list of possible questions you could use during the interview; however, feel free to add or substitute questions of your own.

1. How did you decide on your major field? What influenced your initial decision or attracted you to it in the first place?

Exercise

2. What personal interests, learning styles, or types of intelligence provide a good "match" or "fit" with your field of study?

3. What particular courses in your major did you find especially enjoyable, exciting, or stimulating?

4. What other fields of study relate to your major field and are important for getting a more complete understanding of your field?

5. For students who major in your field, what type of careers do they tend to pursue?

After the interview, answer the following question:

What was the most useful, interesting, or surprising thing I learned about the professor's field, the professor, or myself as a result of conducting this interview?

Conclusion and Farewell

It is our hope that the ideas presented in this book will allow you to see the "big picture," excite you about experiencing the liberal arts and diversity, and prepare you to make the most of these related components on of your college education.

Although you are now just beginning your college experience, when you graduate you will find that your college graduation ceremony is also called *commencement*. It's called that because your college graduation doesn't mark the end of your education; instead it represents the start (commencement) of a lifelong process of learning and personal development whose roots lie in your early college experience with the liberal arts. The broad-based knowledge, versatile skills, and multiple perspectives acquired from the liberal arts—particularly if they are infused with diversity—will be used throughout your life to promote your growth and success and contribute to the growth and success of others with whom you live and work.

It could be said that your life after college will follow a pattern similar to that of the Chinese bamboo tree. The first four years of this tree's growth takes place underground, after which it emerges and grows as high as eighty feet (42). Similarly, your four years in college—grounded in the liberal arts and diversity—provide the underlying roots for lifelong learning and personal growth. We hope that your growth continues until you reach and exceed your highest dreams.

Sincerely,
Joe Cuseo and Aaron Thompson

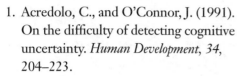

References

1. Acredolo, C., and O'Connor, J. (1991). On the difficulty of detecting cognitive uncertainty. *Human Development, 34,* 204–223.

2. Adelman, C. (2004). Global preparedness of pre-9/11 college graduates: What the U.S. longitudinal studies say. *Tertiary Education and Management, 10,* p. 243.

3. Allport. G. W. (1954). *The nature of prejudice.* Cambridge, MA: Addison-Wesley.

4. Allport, G. W. (1979). *The nature of prejudice* (3rd ed.). Reading, MA: Addison-Wesley.

5. Amir, Y. (1969). Contact hypothesis in ethnic relations. *Psychological Bulletin, 71,* 319–342.

6. Amir, Y. (1976). The role of intergroup contact in change of prejudice and ethnic relations. In P. A. Katz (Ed.), *Towards the elimination of racism* (pp. 245–308). New York: Pergamon Press.

7. Anderson, M. and Fienberg, S. E. (2000). Race and ethnicity and the controversy over the U.S. census. *Current Sociology, 48*(3), 87–110.

8. Applebee, A. N. (1984). Writing and reasoning. *Review of Educational Research, 54*(4), 577–596.

9. Aronson, E., Wilson, T. D., and Akert, R. M. (2007). *Social psychology.* Upper Saddle River, NJ: Pearson/Prentice Hall.

10. Association of American Colleges and Universities (2002). *Greater expectations: The commitment to quality as a nation goes to college.* Washington, DC: Author.

11. Association of American Colleges and Universities (2007). *College learning for the new global century.* A report from the National Leadership Council for Liberal Education and America's Promise. Washington, DC: Association of American Colleges and Universities.

12. Astin, A. W. (1993). *What matters in college?* San Francisco: Jossey-Bass.

13. Astin, A. W., Vogelgesang, L. J., Ikeda, E. K., Yee, J. A. (2000). *How service-learning affects students.* Higher Education Research Institute, University of California, Los Angeles.

14. Baer, J. M. (1993). *Creativity and divergent thinking.* Hillsdale, NJ: Erlbaum.

15. Baron, R. A., Byrne, D., and Brauscombe, N. R. (2006). *Social psychology* (11th ed.). Boston: Pearson.

16. Bass, B. M. and Riggio, R. E. (2005). *Transformational leadership* (2nd ed.). Mahwah, NJ: Lawrence Erlbaum Associates.

17. Belenky, M. F., Clinchy, B., Goldberger, N. R., and Tarule, J. M. (1986). *Women's ways of knowing: The development of self, voice, and mind.* New York: Basic Books.

18. Bellah, R. N., Madsen, R., Sullivan, W. M., Swidler, A., and Tipton, S. M. (1985). *Habits of the heart: Individualism and commitment in American life.* Berkeley: University of California Press.

19. Bishop, S. (1986). Education for political freedom. *Liberal Education, 72*(4), 322–325.

20. Blair, I. V. (2002). The malleability of automatic stereotypes and prejudice.

Personality and Social Psychology Review, 6(3), 242–261.

21. Bligh, D. A. (2000). *What's the use of lectures.* San Francisco: Jossey-Bass.

22. Bloch, B. (1995). Career enhancement through foreign language skills. *International Journal of Career Management, 7*(6), 15–26.

23. Bok, D. (2006). *Our underachieving colleges.* Princeton, NJ: Princeton University Press.

24. Bowen, H. R. (1977). *Investment in learning: The individual and social value of American higher education.* San Francisco: Jossey-Bass.

25. Bowen, H. R. (1997). *Investment in learning: The individual and social value of American higher education* (2nd ed.). Baltimore: The Johns Hopkins Press.

26. Braskamp, L. A. (2008). Developing global citizens. *Journal of College and Character, 10*(1), 1–5.

27. Bridgeman, B. (2003). *Psychology and evolution: The Origins of mind.* Thousand Oaks, CA: Sage.

28. Broadbent, D. E. (1970). Review lecture. *Proceedings of the Royal Society of London B,* 333–350.

29. Brookings Institute (2008). *Demographic keys to the 2008 election.* Washington, DC: Brooking Institute. Retrieved January 3, 2009, from www.brookings.edu/~/media/Files/events/2008/1020_demographic/20081020_demographics.pdf

30. Brown, D. (2003). *Career information, career counseling, and career development* (8th ed.). Boston: Allyn & Bacon.

31. Brown, T. D., Dane, F. C., and Durham, M. D. (1998). Perception of race and ethnicity. *Journal of Social Behavior and Personality, 13*(2), 295–306.

32. Business-Higher Education Forum (1999). *Spanning the chasm: A blueprint for action.* Washington, DC: Author.

33. Business-Higher Education Forum (2002). Investing in people: Developing all of America's talent on campus and in the workplace. Washington, DC: Author.

34. Caplan, P. J., and Caplan, J. B. (1994). *Thinking critically about research on sex and gender.* New York: HarperCollins College Publishers.

35. Carlson, J. S., Burn, B. B., Useem, J., and Yachimowicz, D. (1990). *Study abroad: The experience of American undergraduates.* New York: Greenwood Press.

36. Cianciotto, J. (2005). *Hispanic and Latino same-sex couple households in the United States: A report from the 2000 Census.* New York: The National Gay and Lesbian Task Force Policy Institute and the National Latino/a Coalition for Justice.

37. Colombo, G., Cullen, R., and Lisle, B. (1995). *Rereading America: Cultural contexts for critical thinking and writing.* Boston: Bedford Books of St. Martin's Press.

38. Congressional Commission on the Advancement of Women in Minorities in Science, Engineering and Technology Development (2000). *Land of plenty: Diversity as America's competitive edge in science, engineering and technology.* Retrieved April 12, 2009, from http://www.nsf.gov/pubs/2000/cawmset0409/cawmset_0409.pdf

39. Conley, D. T. (2005). *College knowledge: What it really takes for students to succeed and what we can do to get them ready.* San Francisco: Jossey-Bass.

40. Cook, S. W. (1984). Cooperative interaction in multiethnic contexts. In N. B. Miller and M. B. Brewer (Eds.), *Groups in contact: The psychology of desegregation.* New York: Academic Press.

41. Covey, S. R. (1990). *Seven habits of highly effective people* (2nd ed). New York: Fireside.

42. Covey, S. R., Merrill, A. R., and Merrill, R. R. (1996). *First things first: To live, to love, to learn, to leave a legacy*. New York: Fireside.

43. Cronon, W. (1998). "Only Connect": The Goals of a Liberal Education. *The American Scholar (Autumn)*, 73–80.

44. Cross, K. P. (1982). Thirty years passed: Trends in general education. In B. L. Johnson (Ed.), *General education in two-year colleges* (pp. 11–20). San Francisco: Jossey-Bass.

45. Cummings, M. C. (2002). *Democracy under pressure* (9th ed.). Belmont, CA: Wadsworth.

46. Cuseo, J. B. (1996). *Cooperative learning: A pedagogy for addressing contemporary challenges and critical issues in higher education*. Stillwater, OK: New Forums Press.

47. Cuseo, J. B. (1998). Objectives and benefits of senior year programs. In J. N. Gardner, and G. Van der Veer (Eds.), *The senior year experience: Facilitating integration, reflection, closure, and transition* (pp. 21–36). San Francisco: Jossey-Bass.

48. Dalton, J. C., Eberhardt, D., Bracken, J., and Echols, K. (2006). Inward journeys: Forms and patterns of college student spirituality. *Journal of College and Character*, 7(8), 1–21. Retrieved December 17, 2006, from http://www.collegevalues.org/pdfs/Dalton.pdf

49. Donald, J. G. (2002). *Learning to think: Disciplinary perspectives*. San Francisco: Jossey-Bass.

50. Dryden, G. and Vos, J. (1999). *The learning revolution: To change the way the world learns*. Torrance, CA and Auckland, New Zealand: The Learning Web.

51. Dupuy, G. M., and Vance, R. M. (1996, Oct. 26). *Launching your career: A transition module for seniors*. Paper presented at the Second National Conference on Students in Transition, San Antonio, Texas.

52. Eble, K. E. (1966). *A perfect education* pp. 241–215. New York: Macmillan.

53. Education Commission of the States (1995). *Making quality count in undergraduate education*. Denver, CO: ECS Distribution Center.

54. Elder, L., and Paul, R. (2002). *The miniature guide to taking charge of the human mind*. Dillon Beach, CA: The Foundation for Critical Thinking.

55. Encrenaz, T., Bibring, J. P., Blanc M., Barucci, M. A., Roques, F. and Zarka, P. (2004). *The solar system*. Berlin, Germany: Springer.

56. Family Care Foundation (2005). *If the world were a village of 100 people*. Retrieved December 19, 2006, from http:www.familycare.org.news/if_the_world.htm

57. Feagin, J. R., and Feagin, C. (2003). *Racial and ethnic relations*. Upper Saddler River, NJ: Prentice Hall.

58. Feldman, K. A., and Newcomb, T. M. (1994). *The impact of college on students*. New Brunswick, NJ: Transaction Publishers (originally published in 1969 by Jossey-Bass).

59. Fixman, C. S. (1990). The foreign language needs of U.S.-based corporations. *Annals of the American Academy of Political and Social Science, 511*, 25–46.

60. Ford, P. L. (Ed.) (1903). *The works of Thomas Jefferson*. New York: Knickerbocker Press.

61. Franklin, K. F. (2002. Conversations with Metropolitan University first-year students. *Journal of the First-Year Experience and Students in Transition, 14*(2), 57–88.

62. Gamson, Z. F. (1984). *Liberating education*. San Francisco: Jossey-Bass.

63. Gardner, H. (1999). *Intelligence reframed: Multiple intelligences for the twenty-first century*. New York: Basic Books.

64. Glassman, J. K. (2000, June 9). The technology revolution: Road to freedom or road to serfdom? *Heritage Lectures*, No. 668. Washington, DC: The Heritage Foundation.

65. Goleman, D. (1992, Oct. 27). Voters assailed by unfair persuasion. *The New York Times*, pp. C1–C3.

66. Goleman, D. (1995). *Emotional intelligence: Why it can matter more than IQ*. New York: Random House.

67. Goslin, A. (2007–2008). Bored? *Scientific American Mind*, *18*(6), pp. 20–27.

68. Gurin, P. (1999). New research on the benefits of diversity in college and beyond: An empirical analysis. *Diversity Digest* (spring). Retrieved November 21, 2008 from http://www.diversityweb.org/Digest/Sp99/benefits.html

69. Heath, H. (1976). What the enduring effects of higher education tell us about liberal education. *Journal of Higher Education*, *47*, 173–190.

70. Heath, H. (1977). *Maturity and competence: A transcultural view*. New York: Halsted Press.

71. Herman, R. E. (2000). Liberal arts: The key to the future. *USA Today Magazine* (November), *129*, p. 34.

72. Hersh, R. (1994). What our publics want, but think they don't get, from a liberal arts education: Ted Marchese interviews Richard Hersh. *AAHE Bulletin* (November), pp. 8–10.

73. Hersh, R. (1997). Intentions and perceptions: A national survey of public attitudes toward liberal arts education. *Change*, *29*(2), pp. 16–23.

74. Indiana University (2004). *Selling your liberal arts degree to employers*. Bloomington, IN: Indiana University, Arts and Sciences Placement Office. Retrieved July 7, 2004, from http://www.indiana.edu/~career/fulltime/selling_liberal_arts.html

75. Jablonski, N. G., and Chaplin, G. (2002). Skin deep. *Scientific American* (October), 75–81.

76. Janis, I. L. (1982). *Groupthink: Psychological studies of policy decisions and fiascoes*. (2nd ed.). Boston: Houghton Mifflin.

77. Joint Science Academies Statement (2005). *Global response to climate change*. Retrieved August 29, 2005, from http://nationalacademies.org/onpi/06072005.pdf

78. Katz, J., and Henry, M. (1993). *Turning professors into teachers: A new approach to faculty development and student learning*. Phoenix: American Council on Education and Oryx Press.

79. Kaufman, J. C., and Baer, J. (2002). Could Steven Spielberg manage the Yankees? Creative thinking in different domains. *Korean Journal of Thinking and Problem Solving*, *12*(2), 5–14.

80. Kaufmann, N. L., Martin, J. M., and Weaver, H. D. (1992). *Students abroad: Strangers at home: Education for a global society*. Yarmouth, ME: Intercultural Press, 1992.

81. Kearns, D. (1989). Getting schools back on track. *Newsweek* (November), pp. 8–9.

82. King, P. N., Brown, M. K., Lindsay, N. K., and Vanhencke, J. R. (2007). Liberal arts student learning outcomes: An integrated approach. *About Campus*, September/October, pp. 2–9.

83. Kitchener, K., Wood, P., and Jensen, L. (2000, August). *Curricular, co-curricular, and institutional influence on real-world problem-solving*. Paper presented at the annual meeting of the American Psychological Association, Boston.

84. Knoll, A. H. (2003). *Life on a young planet: The first three billion years of evolution on earth*. Princeton, NJ: Princeton University Press.

85. Kuh, G. D. (1995). The other curriculum: Out-of-class experiences associated with student learning and personal development. *Journal of Higher Education, 66*(2), 123–153.

86. Kuh, G. D., Douglas, K. B., Lund, J. P., and Ramin-Gyurnek, J. (1994). *Student learning outside the classroom: Transcending artificial boundaries*. ASHE-ERIC Higher Education Report, No. 8. Washington, D.C.: George Washington University, School of Education and Human Development.

87. Kuh, G. D., Shedd, J. D., and Whitt, E. H. (1987). Student affairs and liberal education: Unrecognized (and unappreciated) common law partners. *Journal of College Student Personnel, 28*(3), 252–259.

88. Kurfiss, J. G. (1988). *Critical thinking: theory, research, practice, and possibilities*. ASHE-ERIC, Report No. 2. Washington, DC: Association for the Study of Higher Education.

89. Lancaster and Stillman (2002). *When generations collide*. New York, NY: Harper Collins.

90. Langer, J. A., and Applebee, A. N. (1987). *How writing shapes thinking*. NCTE Research Report No. 22. Urbana, IL: National Council of Teachers of English.

91. LeBaron, M. (2003). *Bridging cultural conflicts: New approaches for a changing world*. San Francisco: Jossey-Bass.

92. Levin, D. T. (2000). Race as a visual feature: Using visual search and perceptual discrimination tasks to understand face categories and the cross-race recognition deficit. *Journal of Experimental Psychology: General, 129,* 559–574.

93. Light, R. J. (2001). *Making the most of college: Students speak their minds*. Cambridge, MA: Harvard University Press.

94. Locks, A. M., Hurtado, S., Bowman, N., and Osequera, L. (2008). Extending notions of campus climate and diversity to students' transition to college. *Review of Higher Education, 31*(3), 257–285.

95. Lopez, G. E., Gurin, P., and Nagda, B. A. (1998). Education and understanding structural causes for group inequalities. *Journal of Political Psychology, 19*(2), 305–329.

96. Lott, B. (2002). Cognitive and behavior distancing from the poor. *American Psychologist, 57,* 100–110.

97. Love, P., and Love, A. G. (1995). *Enhancing student learning: Intellectual, social, and emotional integration*. ASHE-ERIC Higher Education Report No. 4. Washington, D.C.: The George Washington University. Graduate School of Education and Human Development.

98. Mackes (2003). Employers describe perfect job candidate. *NACEWeb Press Releases*. Retrieved July 13, 2004, from http://www.naceweb.org/press

99. Magolda, M. B. B. (1992). *Knowing and reasoning in college*. San Francisco: Jossey-Bass.

100. Massey, D. (2003). *The source of the river: The social origins of freshmen at America's selective colleges and universities*. Princeton, NJ: Princeton University Press.

101. Matlock, J. (1997). Student expectations and experiences: The Michigan study. *Diversity Digest* (summer). Retrieved November 21, 2008 from, http://www.diversityweb.org/Digest/Sm97/research.html

102. McCabe, D., and Arp, D. (2009). Do the liberal arts still matter? *Chapman Magazine, fall,* 24–27.

103. Miller, G. (1988). *The meaning of general education*. New York: Teachers College Press.

104. Miville, M. L., Molla, B., and Sedlacek, W. E. (1992). Attitudes of tolerances for diversity among college students. *Journal of the Freshman Year Experience, 4*(1), 95–110.

105. Molnar, S. (1991). *Human variation: race, type, and ethnic groups* (3rd ed.). Englewood Cliffs, NJ: Prentice-Hall.

106. Myers, D. G. (1993). *The pursuit of happiness: Who is happy—and why?* New York: Morrow.

107. Myers, N. (1997). The rich diversity of biodiversity issues. In M. L. Reaka-Kudla, D. E. Wilson, and E. O. Wilson (Eds.), *Biological diversity II: Understanding and protecting our biological resources* (pp. 125–134). National Academic of Sciences, Washington, D.C.: Joseph Henry Press.

108. Nagda, B. R., Gurin, P., and Johnson, S. M. (2005). Living, doing and thinking diversity: How does pre-college diversity experience affect first-year students' engagement with college diversity? In R. S. Feldman (Ed.), *Improving the first year of college: Research and practice* (pp. 73–110). Mahwah, NJ: Lawrence Erlbaum Associates.

109. Nagda, B. R., Gurin, P., and Lopez, G. E. (2003). Transformative pedagogy for democracy and social justice. *Race, Ethnicity, and Education, 6*(2), 165–191.

110. Naisbitt, J. (1982). *Megatrends: Ten new directions transforming our lives.* New York: Warner Books.

111. National Association of Colleges and Employers (NACE) (2003). *Job outlook 2003 survey.* Bethlehem, PA: Author.

112. National Committee on Pay Equity (2008). *The wage gap over time: In real dollars, women see a continuing gap.* Retrieved October 1, 2008, from http:www.pay-equity.org/info-time.html

113. National Resources Defense Council (2005). *Global warming: A summary of recent findings on the changing global climate.* Retrieved Nov. 11, 2005, from http://www.nrdc.org/global/Warming/fgwscience.asp

114. National Survey of Voters (1998). *Autumn overview report conducted by DYG Inc.* Retrieved July 15, 2004, from htttp://www.diversityweb.org/research_and_trends/research_evaluation_impact_/campus_community_ connections/national_poll.cfm

115. National Women's Law Center (2007). *Congress must act to close the wage gap for women.* Retrieved October, 2008, from http://www.pay-equity.org/PDFs?PaycheckFarirnessAct_2007.pdf

116. Newman, J. H. (1852). *The idea of a university.* (Reprinted 1907). New York, NY: Longmans, Green, & Co.

117. Nicholas, R. W. (1991). Cultures in the curriculum. *Liberal Education, 77*(3), 16–21.

118. Niles, S. G., and Harris-Bowlsbey, J. (2002). *Career development interventions in the twenty-first century.* Upper Saddle River, NJ: Pearson Education.

119. Norse, E. A. (1990). *The wilderness society.* Washington, DC: Island Press.

120. Novinger, T. (2001). *Intercultural communication: A practical guide.* Austin, TX: University of Texas Press.

121. Obama, B. (2006). *The audacity of hope: Thoughts on reclaiming the American dream.* New York: Three Rivers Press.

122. Office of Research (1994). *What employers expect of college graduates: International knowledge and second language skills.* Washington, D.C.: Office of Educational Research and Improvement (OERI), U.S. Department of Education.

123. Oller, D. K. (1981). Infant vocalizations: Exploration and reflectivity. In R. E. Stark (Ed.), *Language behavior in infancy and early childhood* (pp. 85–104). New York: Elsevier/North-Holland.

124. Pascarella, E. T. (2001). Cognitive growth in college: Surprising and reassuring findings from The National Study of Student Learning. *Change* (November/December), 21–27.

125. Pascarella, E., Palmer, B., Moye, M., and Pierson, C. (2001). Do diversity experiences influence the development of critical thinking? *Journal of College Student Development, 42,* 257–291.

126. Pascarella, E. and Terenzini, P. (1991). *How college affects students: Findings and insights from twenty years of research.* San Francisco: Jossey-Bass.

127. Pascarella, E. T., and Terenzini, P. T. (2005). *How college affects students: A third decade of research* (volume 2). San Francisco: Jossey-Bass.

128. Paul, R. W., and Elder, L. (2002). *Critical thinking: Tools for taking charge of your professional and personal life.* Upper Saddle River, NJ: Pearson Education.

129. Peter D. Hart Research Associates (2006). *How should college prepare students to succeed in today's global economy?* Washington, D.C.: American Association of Colleges and Universities.

130. Pettigrew, T. F. (1997). Generalized intergroup contact effects on prejudice. *Personality and Social Psychology Bulletin, 23,* 173–185.

131. Pinker, S. (1994). *The language instinct.* New York: HarperCollins.

132. Pratto, F., Liu, J. H., Levin, S., Sidanius, J., Shih, M., Bachrach, H., and Hegarty, P. (2000). Social dominance orientation and the legitimization of inequality across cultures. *Journal of Cross-Cultural Psychology, 31,* 369–409.

133. Ramsey, R. J., and Frank, J. (2007). Wrongful conviction. *Crime and Delinquency, 53*(3), 436–470.

134. Ratcliff, J. L. (1997). What is a curriculum and what should it be? In J. G. Gaff, J. L Ratcliff, and Associates, *Handbook of the undergraduate curriculum: A comprehensive guide to purposes, structures, practices, and change* (pp. 5–29). San Francisco: Jossey-Bass.

135. Riquelme, H. (2002). Can people creative in imagery interpret ambiguous figures faster than people less creative in imagery? *Journal of Creative Behavior, 36*(2), 105–116.

136. Rose, S., and Hartmann, H. (2004). *Still a man's labor market: The long-term earnings gap.* Washington, D.C.: The Institute for Women's Policy Research.

137. Rosenberg, M. (2009). *The number of countries in the word.* Retrieved Nov. 18, 2009, from http://geography.about.com/cs/countries/a/numbercountries.htm

138. Sangrigoli, S., Pallier, C., Argenti, A. M., Ventureyra, V. A. G., and de Schonen, S. (2005). Reversibility of the other-race effect in face recognition during childhood. *Psychological Science, 16,* 440–444.

139. Sax, L. J., Lindholm, J. A., Astin, A. W., Korn, W. S., and Mahoney, K. M. (2004). *The American freshman: National norms for fall, 2004.* Los Angeles: Higher Education Research Institute, UCLA.

140. Segall, M. H., Campbell, D. T., and Herskovits, M. J. (1966). The influence of culture on visual perception. Indianapolis: Bobbs-Merrill.

141. Senge, P. (1990). *The fifth dimension.* New York: Currency/Doubleday.

142. Shah, A. (2009). *Global issues: Poverty facts and stats.* Retrieved January 2, 2010, from

http://www.globalissues.org/artoc;e/26/poverty-facts-and-stats

143. Sherif, M., Harvey, D. J., White, B. J., Hood, W. R., and Sherif, C. W. (1961). *The robbers' cave experiment.* Norman, OK: Institute of Group Relations.

144. Sidanius, J., Levin, S., Liu, H., and Pratto, F. (2000). Social dominance orientation, antiegalitarianism, and the political psychology of gender: An extension and cross-cultural replication. *European Journal of Social Psychology, 30,* 41–67.

145. Smith, D. (1997). How diversity influences learning. *Liberal Education, 83*(2), 42–48.

146. Stangor, C., Sechrist, G. B., and Jost, T. J. (2001). Changing racial beliefs by providing consensus information. *Personality and Social Psychology Bulletin, 27,* 486–496.

147. Strage, A. A. (2000). Service-learning: Enhancing student learning outcomes in a college-level course. *Michigan Journal of Community Service Learning, 7,* 5–13.

148. Terenzini, P. T., and Pascarella, E. T. (2004, July). *How college affects students: A third decade of research.* Plenary address to the Academic Affairs Summer Conference of the American Association of State Colleges and Universities. Albuquerque, New Mexico.

149. The Board of Trustees of the University of Illinois (2005). *Career Preparation.* College of Liberal Arts & Sciences, University of Illinois at Urbana Champaign. Retrieved December 16, 2006, from http://www.las.uiuc.edu/students/career/businesscareers.html

150. The Conference Board of Canada (2000). *Employability skills 2000+.* Ottawa: The Conference Board of Canada.

151. Torres, V. (2003). Student diversity and academic services: Balancing the needs of all students. In G. L. Kramer & Associates, *Student academic services: An integrated approach* (pp. 333–352). San Francisco: Jossey-Bass.

152. UN New Centre (2010, January 1). *UN opens biodiversity year with plea to save world's ecosystems.* Retrieved January 11, 2010, from http://www.un.org/apps/news/story.asp?NewsID=33393&CR=environmnet&Cr1

153. University of New Hampshire Office of Residential Life (2001). *The hate that hate produced.* Retrieved January 8, 2007, from http:/www.unh.edu/residential-life/diversity/kn_articles6.pdf

154. U.S. Census Bureau (2000). *Racial and ethnic classifications in Census 2000 and beyond.* Retrieved December 19, 2006, from http://census.gov/population/www/socdemo/race/racefactcb.html

155. U.S. Census Bureau (2004). *The face of our population.* Retrieved December 12, 2006, from http://factfinder.census.gov/jsp/saff/SAFFInfojsp?_pageId=tp9_race_ethnicity

156. U.S. Census Bureau (2008). Current Population Survey Annual Social and Economic Supplement. Washington, DC: Author.

157. Useem, M. (1989). *Liberal education and the corporation: The hiring and advancement of college graduates.* Edison, NJ: Aldine Transaction.

158. "Voices" (2009). Whither the liberal arts? *Chapman Magazine,* fall, p. 36.

159. Wabash National Study of Liberal Arts Education (2007). *Liberal Arts outcomes.* Retrieved December 18, 2009, from http:www.liberalarts.wabash.edu/study-overview/

160. Watts, M. M. (2005). The place of the library versus the library as place. In M. L. Upcraft, J. N. Gardner, and

B. O. Barefoot & Associates, *Challenging and supporting the first-year student* (pp. 339–355). San Francisco: Jossey-Bass.

161. Wheelright, J. (2005). Human, study thyself. *Discover* (March), pp. 39–45.

162. Wilder, D. A. (1984). Inter-group contact: The typical member and the exception to the rule. *Journal of Experimental Psychology, 20,* 177–194.

163. Zajonc, R. B. (2001). Mere exposure: A gateway to the subliminal. *Current Directions in Psychological Science, 10,* 224–228.

164. Zernike, K. (2009). Making college 'relevant.' *The New York Times, Education Life,* December 29. Retrieved January 4, 2010, from http://nytimes.com/2010/01/03education/edlife/03careerism-t.html

165. Zohar, D., and Marshall, I. (2000). *SQ: Connecting with your spiritual intelligence.* New York: Bloomsbury.